GROWING
THE
CHURCH

GARY VICKERY

ISBN 978-1-0980-7515-6 (paperback)
ISBN 978-1-0980-7516-3 (digital)

Christian Faith Publishing, Inc.
832 Park Avenue
Meadville, PA 16335
www.christianfaithpublishing.com

Printed in the United States of America

Contents

Introduction

This book was written because of my love for the church, the "bride of Christ," and because for the last forty years, I have seen a dramatic decline in church attendance. I have listed several reasons for this decline in this book as well as some hopeful cures and medications, to not only get the church back to surviving but also to grow it back into the healthy church I grew up in, and that was one in which sometimes it was standing room when all the pews were filled.

This book was not written as a duty but because of the total love that I have for God's church and for the people that make up the church. I would love to see full churches again and to experience the fellowship with everyone.

This can be done if we make sure that every Christian does a complete change from being a spectator to being someone that will get in the game, get on the field, get a little muddy and dirty, and play to win souls.

I hope you enjoy reading this book as much as I enjoyed writing it. This was not work to me but simply being a Christian and sharing my blessings.

In Christian love, I remain.
Gary Vickery
Garvic59@yahoo.com

For speaking engagements, please email your phone number.

Winning Souls

Winning souls can be the most satisfying accomplishment of your life; however, it does take some effort, and for every soul you help lead to Christ, you will add another star to your crown. I cannot imagine anything more important than seeing and talking to people that you have helped avoid hell when you get to heaven. You and these souls that you have helped to convert will be singing to the Highest, and it will last forever. Just think about it, when you've been there ten million years, it's just beginning. No sadness, no crying, no loneliness, no sickness, no hurting, just you and all the people that you loved on earth that, because of you, decided to live a Christian life, including family and friends and complete strangers that maybe you influenced along the way. This life, even if you live to an old age, is so short and temporary compared to forever, and even if you are very successful and make a lot of money while here, it is nothing compared to what you will see and do in the next life. Your heart will, at some time, stop beating; however, you will continue to live in one of two places. Heaven or hell, the choice is yours because you are already in your journey to eternity. It's up to you to decide and you will miss out on all the fun if you make the wrong decision.

If we are to grow the church and win people to Christianity, then we have to become involved in order for it to work. The fruit of the Spirit is a result of God living in us, and when He does, we produce characteristics that could never exist unless he is present. The fruit of the Spirit is God in you and to know that God is good. "How abundant is Your goodness, which You have stored up for those who love You, to those who take refuge in You (Ps. 31:19)." We need to conform to His image, and in conforming to His image, we will become the likeness of His goodness, His mercy, and His being. This doesn't speak of having an attitude as much as it speaks of having a new lifestyle that shows helpfulness, doing good to others, and considering others before yourself.

Generosity shows that your lifestyle is not about your money and personal possessions but what is in your heart. We have to become proactive in serving others.

We start by visiting the sick, giving to the poor, caring for the widows and orphans, helping the homeless, loving our enemies, praying for the lost, sharing Jesus, lifting up the weak and fallen, showing forgiveness, bearing one another's burdens, being kind to everyone, and showing hospitality. These are just a few of the acts that are required to win souls.

It is easy to make excuses for ourselves to keep from being generous to others because we are not rich, but the list above has nothing to do with having a lot of money. Goodness is not about the amount but is about the moment. Look around during the day and see what God has placed in our hand. Who do we see that God has placed before us that we can selflessly serve? It doesn't take any more effort to be nice than it does to ignore and walk away.

There is a story in Matthew chapter 12, where we catch a glimpse of goodness at work. Jesus was opposite the place where the offerings were put and watched the people put their money into the temple treasury. Lots of rich people threw in large amounts, but a widow came by and put in two small copper coins, two pennies, that was worth only a fraction of the amount of the others, and Jesus called His disciples to Him and said, "I tell you the truth, this poor widow has put more into the treasury than all the others. They all gave out of their wealth, but she didn't give just one and keep one. She gave both, and it's called *sacrificial generosity*. This is goodness in God's eyes."

People will forget what we say and some might forget what we did, but people will never forget how we made them feel with our generous goodness. Ralph Waldo Emerson said, "We cannot show kindness too soon, for we never know how soon it will be too late."

You are the salt of the earth. You are the light of the world. Let your light shine before men that they may see your good deeds and praise your Father in heaven.

You never know when you are going to influence someone, will it be a good influence or a bad one. It's an awesome responsibility to watch out how we influence someone. Most of us are guilty of thinking we have little or no influence, but this is not true. We all influence others around us. It's our choice of how we will affect the lives of others, either for good or bad. We can't remain neutral. It's not an option for any one of us. In Romans 14:7, Paul said, "None of us lives to himself alone and none of us dies to himself alone." Everyone has some kind of influence over others, everyone.

Here is just a few of how some people influenced others… Eve influenced the one she loved the most to sin. The people of Israel influenced Aaron, Moses's brother, to build the golden calf. The ten spies used their influence to destroy the faith of Israel. Absalom used his power of influence to incite a revolt against his own father, David. The Samaritan woman influenced an entire city: "Come see the Messiah."

We all have and do influence people all the time. We can't stop it. All we can do is try to control it, shape it, and if needed, change it. What we cannot do is turn it off. The bottom line is, our influence is active, powerful, and working every minute whether we are conscious of this fact or not. So let us always be mindful of how we can be effective stewards of our influence.

As Christian, we have to watch our character. We are to be different people, and we are to have the mind and manners of Jesus. His thoughts and behavior need to become our way of thinking and acting. Character influences, and a Jesus character influences for good every time, every time.

I have to say that, regardless of what we say and how we say it, if people catch even a glimpse of insincerity in our speech or behavior, our influence will take a nosedive into the negative and might cause people to misunderstand us.

Church (we will get more into church later in this book), our motive is everything. We all have to be a person of pure motive. Listen to Jesus: "These people honor me with their lips, but their hearts are far from me" (Matt. 15:8). "Blessed are the pure in Heart, for they shall see God" (Matt. 5:8). Here it is church, we are what we think, not just what we say or do. Solomon wrote, "As a man thinks in his heart, so is he" (Prov. 23:7). The problem is that people around us can sense what's in our heart. People see through our improper motives. A Christ-like influence demands that we correct our motives. In effect, Jesus said, "Don't pray, give your alms, or fast to be seen of others." If we have the correct motives, it will enhance our influence and make us right with God.

Jesus was a people person, and He taught that people were more important than law. The Sabbath was made for man, not man for the Sabbath (Mark 2–27). Jesus taught that we must love others, all others! For God so loved the world that He sent His one and only Son. We must stop choosing to love some and hate others. Hate was not in the heart of Jesus, and neither should it be in ours. We have to hold people above all other earthly things, because God does. Our influence, even our relationship with God, is dependent upon our relationship with our fellowman.

Influence demands consistency, and anybody can do anything right once, but those of us who have named Christ as our Lord and Savior must strive for a Jesus character. We have to love others and be consistently consistent because inconsistency destroys influence.

We Are All Ambassadors of the King

We have all been given a mission, and it began when we read about the Great Commission (Matt. 10:14–16), and we hear Jesus telling us to "go and make disciples." So we can see that God has given us a job to do, and it is God's plan that we are to be His ambassador and work. That work begins in the church, because it is through individuals within the church that wins souls to God, and it is His plan that we are to work.

The question that always seems to come up is "How?" We can find one answer by looking at something else we read in Luke chapter 10, where Luke records the sending out of the seventy-two. We are to be totally reliant on God. Listen to what Jesus tells the seventy-two in Luke 10:3–4: "Go your way, behold, I am sending you out as lambs in the midst of wolves, carry no moneybag, no knapsack, no sandals, and greet no one on the road." What He is saying is not to be concerned with personal needs and don't stop and lose a lot of time with aimless talk along the way. Lambs in the midst of wolves speak about how we are defenseless and our vulnerable. Not worrying too much about personal things along the way is demonstrating our faith in the fact that God can and will take care of us. When we read the Gospel accounts of Jesus calling His followers, we hear Him say things like "Come and see" or "Come follow me." He didn't lay out a long plan for people. He asked them to trust Him to lead. We don't always know what the future holds, but we need to know and trust in the One who does. Faith in God is a vital part of our mission.

When we are out and about God's work and we speak to someone and have a smile for them and if they smile back and are kind, they may be the person that perhaps God is already working on, so you don't have to have the answer to every question. Just tell them what you know and believe and ask them to follow you, and all their questions can and will be answered.

We are to carry one thing, and that is the message of the kingdom of God, and say to them, "The Kingdom of God has come near to you." We are to love and serve the people to whom we are sent and to carry the only message we have, and that is the message of peace and reconciliation that the Gospel brings. We are ambassadors, not salespeople. We have been entrusted with the message of the greatest gift of all, the gift that can take care of our greatest need. We dare not cheapen it.

Encouragement

If encouragement is so important, if it enhances relationships and brings hope, strength, growth, and success to people's lives, then we need to challenge one another to become someone that encourages. Everyone appreciates encouragement. Genuine encouragement is vital for life and relationships. Encouragement is like a breeze on a hot summer day. Encouragement helps us to overcome when we feel overwhelmed. It helps us to succeed rather than sink in failure. Encouragement helps us become a victor rather than be a victim. We all hunger and thirst for encouragement. There is never a time in life when we don't need encouragement. There is never a time when encouragement is not appropriate.

We all need to ask the Lord to make us aware of opportunities for encouraging others. Indeed, opportunities are all around us, but we must train ourselves to look for the possibilities. Look for an open door, encourage, and change a life forever.

We all have to be time sensitive and willing to take the risk. Is there someone in your life that needs encouragement today? What's keeping you from encouraging them? Why are you waiting? Why do you wait? Tomorrow may be too late. Our procrastination could cost someone a soul. Let us not be like Peter and have to have three visions before we encourage others to become participants in God's kingdom. Anytime is the right time to be an encourager. When God opens the door, then we must never allow anything to stop us. Who do we need to encourage this week? Tomorrow? Right now with a phone call, a card, a face-to-face conversation.

The Church

This is a part of God's church. People that made up the early church were taught that they were set apart for a specific purpose and that was to convert everyone they met to be a Christian, which meant to follow Jesus. To be a part of His community, His kingdom. They were called to separate themselves from all the bad things of the world, those who would walk in the light of truth, to be a priesthood of different and peculiar people, those set apart for His purpose, His divine function. "And God placed all things under His feet and made Him to be head over everything for the church" (Eph. 1:22).

Paul is found saying, "I am writing you these instructions so that you know how people ought to conduct themselves in God's household, in God's family, which is part of the living God." Paul's prayer for the church in Ephesus contains these words: "I bow down on my knees unto the Father of our Lord Jesus Christ of whom the whole family in Heaven is named." God's family includes both the saved in heaven and on earth.

His kingdom, which is listed over fifty times in the New Testament and is the most used metaphor for people as a kingdom. The Old Testament spoke of a kingdom coming. Daniel foretold of a time when God would set up a kingdom that would engulf all people and all kingdoms of the earth. John the Baptizer came proclaiming baptisms for the kingdom is at hand. Jesus told Peter that He would build His church and would give Peter the keys to the kingdom. So when we think of a kingdom, it reminds us that someone must be

King, must be in authority, and that's Jesus. And so we must always remember that the church, that Christ is the Head of, should be the most important thing in our life and should be taken very seriously.

The Bible speaks of the church as a gathering of God's people, with it appearing "church" 112 times and is translated "assembly" three times by the King James translators in the New Testament. Now with this in mind, we can conclude that the church is a community of believers in God. Christ loved the church and gave Himself up for her. And that Christ is the head of the church, His body, of which He is the Savior. His blood also flows past us to the end of time forgiving those who would step into its life-giving stream. His blood cleansed the emerging church beginning in Acts chapter 2 and continuing until He comes again. Paul said, "To Him [Jesus], be glory in the church throughout all ages, all generations" (Eph. 3:21).

Speaking of Christ, Paul says, "God is all things under His feet and appointed Him to be head over everything for the church, which is His body" (Eph. 1:22–23).

Paul also writes to Timothy, giving him and us this admonition. "I am writing you these instructions so that you will know how people ought to conduct themselves in Gods household, in God's family, which is the church of the living God" (1 Tim. 3:14–15). Not everyone who says to me, "Lord, Lord," will enter the kingdom of heaven, but only he who does the will of my Father who is in heaven (Matt. 7:21).

Reasons the Church Is in Decline and Why

The older I get, the more I realize how shallow the preaching is in the church today. They preach "canned" lessons with little depth and knowledge of how "souls were won" in the manner of the early church. It is either nonexistent or just wrong. I would love to hear preaching on topics that many brethren have neglected over the years.

One reason why our churches win so few souls is that the preachers, themselves, win so few, and they fail to stir people to win souls. A preacher who does not personally win souls will not make soul winners out of others. One who does not practice soul winning will not preach soul winning very effectively.

Preachers in personal work alone could win far more souls than they and all their congregation now win. Now I'm not just picking on just preachers because the leadership of the church is just as guilty as anything the preacher does or doesn't do. I call it spiritual laziness on both the preacher and the leadership. There is no way to build great soul-winning churches without soul-winning leadership most of all.

We have been taught in the Great Commission, to preach the Gospel to every creature, "that is to every individual." The Great Commission more definitely commands personal soul winning than public preaching to congregations. Churches may hire preachers to preach, but God calls a preacher to win souls.

Is this not the way Jesus did it Himself? Now we know that He preached to great multitudes and I'm sure He saved many souls because of what He preached and not just going through a duty that preachers do today. He won as an individual the woman of Sychar in Samaria at the site of Jacob's well. He won blind Bartimaeus by the roadside near Jericho, and Zacchaeus up a sycamore tree beside the path. He won the woman who was a sinner at the house of Simon the Leper, the woman taken in adultery as she stood shamed and broken before Him. Jesus, the Master Preacher, continually won souls in a one-on-one basis, something most preachers or church leaders do not do today. A preacher or church leader can win souls even when they can't get lost people to attend church services.

Not only should preachers and church leaders talk and visit with sinners to win their soul, they should also look at the church records and make an effort to go and visit the members that have left the flock and find out why they left and try to win them back. This should be done with more than just a onetime visit but as many visits as it takes to win them back. This is especially lacking in most churches today because nobody goes out to find just the one lost sheep that has wandered away. This would be a tried and true method to grow the church, but when the blind is leading the blind, it is rarely done.

Old and young, both men and women, can be trained as soul winners by developing classes to let them know how to approach, what to say, and not be ashamed or because they feel that they might offend. We should be more afraid of offending the Good Lord than friends or strangers that might be lost. Some will say no or just walk away. However, if you just get one to listen and give them the good news, it will all be worth it. Don't give up or become discouraged, because everyone you help to become a Christian, you will be adding stars to your "crown," and besides, if you get laughed at or mocked, maybe they won't put you on a cross and nail you to it. Get the message. Notice the charts to enlighten you.

The Value of a Soul

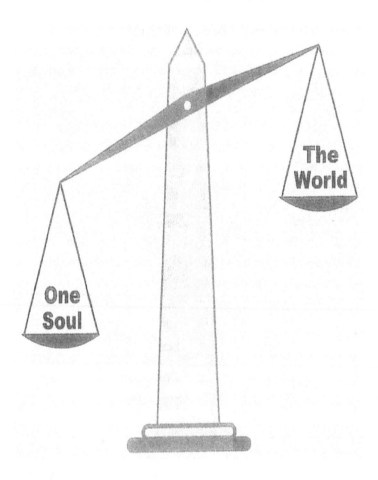

"For what is a man profited if he gains the whole world and loses his soul?" (Matt. 16:26).

One Hundred Sixty-Eight Hours in a Week

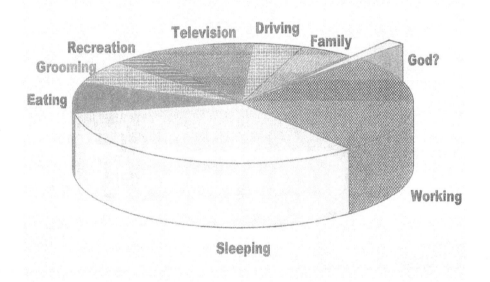

How many are devoted to God?

Why Do People Choose a Church

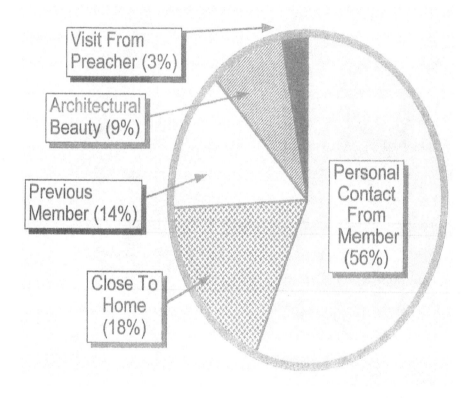

Limiting Factors in Church Growth

If I brought a bucket, or say, a coffee can, up to the pulpit with holes in it from about halfway up and continuing up to the top and asked "How full do you think I can fill this can with water?" what would you say? Well, the answer is obvious, I can fill it up to the area where the holes begin, and then the holes would become our "limiting factor," right? We could dip the can into a bathtub full of water and pull it out, but in a few seconds, the water would fall to the level of the holes. The same principle works in churches. Sometimes our actions are *not* consistent with our beliefs, and then they become limiting factors.

So we have to ask, what are some limiting factors that inhibit church growth?

First, it's possible for a church not *grow spiritually or numerically because of showing a* lack of love.

The first and greatest commandment from the lips of Jesus is found in Matthew 22: *Love God with all your heart, mind, strength, and soul... And the second is like it...love your neighbor as yourself.*

In Matthew 5, Jesus said we were to even *love our enemies...that we may be known as children of God.*

Paul maintained that the fruit produced by the Spirit of God in our lives is *love.* It was Paul who wrote faith, hope, *and love.* But the greatest of these is *love.*

Then he proceeds to tell us what love looks like:

- Love is *patient.*
- Love treats others with *kindness.*
- Love is not *envious* of others.
- It is never found *boasting.*
- Love is not *proud* or *rude.*
- It does not *seek its own way.*
- Is not easily *angered.*
- Love keeps *no record of wrongs…but forgives.*
- Love never *delights in evil but rejoices with the truth.*
- Love always, *always, protects* the of others.
- Love always *trusts.*
- Love always *hopes.*
- Love always *perseveres.*
- *Love never fails.*

Question, which verses describes my life and yours, *really?*

Paul entered this love chapter saying that *as a church or individually…*

- we can appear spiritual by preaching like angels
- be able to quote and understand every Scripture
- and have a faith that could remove mountains

But if we *do not love,* we are nothing.

It was this same Paul who said *our love must be sincere. Be devoted to one another in brotherly love. Honor one another above yourselves.*

A lack of love in a church *is the number one limiting factor to its growth,* spiritually or individually.

In fact, John puts it plainly in these words: *We know that we have passed from* death unto life…*when we love the brethren. He that* loves not *his brother abides in* death.

If a man says "I love God" and hates *his brother, he is lying. For he who* loves not his brother *whom he has seen* cannot love God *whom he not seen. Whoever loves God must love his brother.*

So the question becomes, are we growing in our love for one another? Are we known as a church family who has a warm genuine love for one another? I believe the answer is *yes*... And may a lack of love never become a liability.

The Use of the Tongue

A second limiting factor in church growth is the *use of the tongue.*

One of the greatest *blessings* God has given us is the ability to *communicate.* How we use this ability is up to us.

- We can be known as a *praising, positive, and edifying* church...
- Or as a *murmuring, negative, and complaining* congregation and individual.

Let's examine each of these for a moment, noting what the Bible has to say.

First, in today's culture, it's easy to be known as a *murmuring, negative, and complaining* group or people.

It seems to be America's favorite pastime.

Does Scripture address such an ugly use of the tongue? I believe it does. Listen as we read from Paul in Philippians 2:14–18 (emphasis added):

> Do all things *without murmuring, complaining, and disputing* that you may be blameless and harmless, the sons of God, without rebuke, in the midst of a crooked and perverse nation, among whom you shine lights in the world; holding forth the word of life... Be filled with joy rejoice with me.

Paul is saying...

One, as a church, Christians are to be a *light* shining in an otherwise dark world.

Two, our light, our example, our influence is *enhanced or diminished* by how we deal with life and living. Whether we murmur, complain, and find fault...or whether we are found rejoicing and edifying.

Three, blamelessness and purity in the church of God are dependent upon our ability to control our tongues in this matter of *murmuring and complaining.*

Four, Paul plainly says such use of the tongue is forbidden in the church. *Do all things...in* everything *without complaint.*

This is powerful stuff. Have you ever heard it preached that the purity of each individual Christian, that the purity of each church, is based upon our *not* murmuring, complaining, and disputing?

Did you know this? Murmuring is mentioned more than forty times in the Bible. And every time, it is in a *negative connotation.* Murmuring is *condemned* by God.

- First Corinthians 10:10 states, "Neither murmur did some of Israel and were destroyed."
- James 5:9 states, "Do not grumble or complain against one another."
- Jude 16 defines *murmurs, complainers,* and *fault finders* as "evil and sinful men who walk after their own lust."
- *Why not grumble, murmur, and complain?*
- Because it *discourages* others.
- Because it is *malignant* and *contagious.*

8

That's Gossip

Let's look at another negative of the tongue—*that's gossip.*

Listen to these scriptures:

Proverbs 11:13 states, "A tale bearer reveals secrets, but he that is of a faithful spirit conceals the matter."

Proverbs 26:20 states, "Where there is no wood, the fire is out... So where there is no gossip...strife ceases."

First Timothy 5 states, Speaking of the downfall of young widows, Paul wrote, "They learn to be idle, wandering about from house to house... Not just idle but talebearers...gossips...and busybodies...meddling in other people's business. *This should not be.*"

Let me ask you some questions about *gossip.*

Is it accurate? Do we know that something is true before we pass it on to others?

Is it loving? Will my telling this enhance my relationship with the individual?

Is it the whole picture? Most of the time gossip is taken out of context.

Is it confidential? Some things are true...but should *not* be repeated.

Would this person want me to repeat this? If the answer is no, *don't!*

Is it damaging? Will this individual be better thought of by what I'm about to say?

Would we want this said about us?

Does this need to be shared with those inside or outside the family of God?

Is this really necessary?

Is it something we would be willing to share with Jesus?

Let's turn this stone over and note some Scriptures on the use of the tongue for edifying and building up *the church and everyone in it.*

Listen to these scriptures.

Romans 14:19 states, "Let us make every effort to do what leads to peace and to mutual edification."

First Corinthians 10:23 states, "Everything is permissible... But not everything is beneficial. Everything is permissible. But not everything is constructive. Our Bible says...not everything is edifying."

Ephesians 4:29 states, "Do not let any unwholesome talk come out of your mouths, but only what is helpful for building others up according to their needs."

First Thessalonians 5:11 states, "Encourage one another and build each other up... Just as in fact you are doing."

We must never allow our *lack of tongue control* to become a *limiting factor* in our spiritual or numerical growth. Nobody wants to be a part of a church where the tongue is used in an *abusive manner*. Everybody appreciates and enjoys *edification*.

9

Lack of Commitment

Another limiting factor is an apparent *lack of commitment.*

We've already noticed that our first commitment is to love the Lord with *all we are.* Jesus speaks of commitment in Matthew 6:33: "Seek first his kingdom and his righteousness and all these things will be given to you as well."

We need to, as we go through this life, think about the difference between *a decision and a commitment.* Have we made a *decision* for Jesus...or a *commitment* to Him?

When a couple gets married, they make a *decision.* But that decision may or may not have included a *commitment.* How that marriage turns out is dependent upon whether or not a commitment was involved.

The same is true in the church. You see, the reason the church is *not* making more of an impact on our society is that...

- Many of us made a *decision* about Christ years ago.
- But we have yet to make a *commitment* to Him.

When an airline pilot is speeding down the runway, there is a certain point where staying on the ground is *no longer an option.* When he crosses that line, he's *committed* to the air. A takeoff is a *must* or a crash is imminent.

The challenge by Paul in Romans chapter 12 is to get off the ground. *Make a commitment.* I believe we see commitment in four areas that we'll explore.

The first is a commitment to *personal spiritual growth. I urge you, brothers, in view of God's mercy, to offer your bodies as living sacrifices. Holy and pleasing to God—this is your spiritual act of worship. Do not conform any longer to the pattern of this world, but be transformed by the renewing of your mind. Then you will be able to test and approve what God's will is—his good, pleasing, and perfect will.*

We must know that God has never been satisfied with *dead* sacrifices. What He has always wanted was *living ones.* This was the point made by the Hebrews writer: *Sacrifices and offerings, burnt offerings and sin offerings you did not desire nor were you pleased with them (although the law required them to be made).*

Paul says such a commitment means we must be *transformed in our mind...transformed in heart...*from a worldly way of thinking to a spiritual mind-set. The Greek is *metamorphoo...* The word from which we get our English *metamorphosis.* It speaks of an *inner change* which has *observable outward manifestations.*

The second commitment is to the body...*the* church... *For by the grace given to me, I say to every one of you: Do not think of yourself more highly than you ought but rather think of yourself with sober judgment in accordance with the measure of faith God has given you. Just as each of us has one body with many members and these members do not all have the same function, so in Christ, we who are many form one body. Each member belongs to all the others.*

Our commitment to the local church family is the first level of commitment outside of our personal relationship with the Lord. The local church *with all its imperfections* is still the Lord's body, the *major avenue* through which He accomplishes His word.

Such commitment is *deeper* than just attendance on Sunday morning. We attend church to become *personally involved* in the Lord's work. This commitment demands *loyalty.*

When we find ourselves criticizing the *church family and its leadership or membership or work.* We are shooting ourselves in the foot and cutting off our nose to spite our face.

Paul says our third commitment is *to ministry*. Note verse 6 beginning: *We have different gifts, according to the grace given us. If a man's gift is prophesying, let him use it in to his faith. If it is serving, let him serve; if it is teaching, let him teach; if it is encouraging. let him encourage; if it is contributing to the needs of others, let him give generously; if it is leadership, let him govern diligently; if it is showing mercy, let him it cheerfully. Love must be sincere. Hate what is evil; cling to what is good. Be devoted to one another in brotherly love. Honor one another above yourselves. Never lacking in zeal, but keep your spiritual fervor, serving the Lord. Be joyful in hope, patient in affliction. And faithful in prayer. Share with God's people who are in need. Practice hospitality.*

Ministry is where we put our God-given *gifts, blessings, resources, and abilities to work for the Lord.*

Nowhere in Scripture is it even alluded to that Christianity is a *spectator religion.*

Jesus spoke of the church…the kingdom…

- As a vineyard
- As a field
- As an occupation

Work and Growth

A place where there is both work and growth?

Then finally, Paul says we are be committed to *grow in our relationship with all others*. Bless those who persecute you; bless and do not curse. Rejoice with those rejoice; mourn with those who mourn. Live in harmony with one another. Do not be proud, but be willing to associate with people of low position. Do not be conceited. Do not repay anyone evil for evil. Be careful to do what is right in the eyes of everybody. If it is possible, as far as it depends on you, live at peace with everyone. Do not take revenge, my friends, but leave room for God's wrath, for it is written: "It is mine to avenge; I will repay," says the Lord. On the contrary, "if your enemy is hungry, feed him; if he is thirsty, give him something to drink. In doing this, you will heap burning coals on his head." Do not be overcome by evil, but overcome evil with good.

Where would we find you and your friends?

Do we need to obey the Gospel message, allowing God to add us to the church by *faith…repentance…New Testament baptism?*

Do we need to *love the brethren* more deeply?

Watch the use of our tongue…and be committed to *seek first* His kingdom…His righteousness. It's your choice.

Cultivating a Growth Mentality

I don't know all that the *Holy Spirit* does in the life of a Christian, but I do know *God created us to do good works for ministry*, and He opens doors of opportunity every day for us to become *His instrument of righteousness.*

The question is, will we accept the challenge…walk through those doors of involvement…*or will we quench the spirit?*

I was talking to a friend recently, and out of the blue, he turned and asked me if I had a winning lottery ticket that I would share with him. I said, "No, I don't," and after several seconds, he said, "Well, to win, you first have to buy a ticket." And, so I thought, that is an idea of why the churches don't grow. It is because they don't buy a ticket. They don't do the work that God places before them of encouraging and facilitating those things which growth.

You see, *attitude and expectation define and regulate behavior.*

Churches, including ours, will *not* grow unless and until we have a *growth mentality*…unless we *expect* the growth. Is it possible that we have developed a *maintenance* rather than a *growth* mentality? Regrettably, many of us believe that growing a church is as simple as…

- hiring a reasonably good preacher
- constructing a nice building
- and putting out fires when uncomfortable situations arise
- Here is the real truth…
- A maintenance mentality *does not* grow. *It kills them.*
- Growing churches take a completely different mind-set. It takes a *growth mentality.*

If your church family is to grow in this year, we must remove *maintenance mentality* and replace it with a *growth mentality.*

We must cultivate those attitudes and expectations that promote growth.

Come, let's see what we can learn about cultivating a growth mentality.

A maintenance mentality relies on us.

A growth mentality relies on God.

Paul explained how church growth works in 1 Corinthians 3:6–7: "I planted the seed, Apollos watered it, but God makes it grow. So neither he who plants nor he who waters is anything, but only God, who makes things grow."

Then there is an interesting phrase in Colossians 2:19, where Paul says it's possible for us to lose connection with the head of the church...*which causes it to grow.* Paul indicates that *church growth is facilitated by God...by Christ!*

- It is true that *we work... We buy the ticket!*
- *But God causes the growth.*

Church, we must recognize this premise as the basis for any possible progress we can ever expect to make. While those with a maintenance mentality *think* about the work we need to do...

- And spend most of their time being *overwhelmed* because there is so much that needs to be done.
- Remember what 2 Corinthians 5:7 (emphasis added) says, "*We walk by faith...not by sight.*"
- Maintenance churches walk and work by *sight...by what they know.*
- Growth churches walk and work by *faith...by doing their work and trusting God's promised increase.*

Believing if we *plant, water, and cultivate,* God will give the increase. Can you imagine what our church family would look like if we *walked by faith* instead of by sight?

Maintenance or Growth Mentality

A maintenance mentality is satisfied.
  A growth mentality is constructively discontent.
  Maintainers are *satisfied with good enough.*

- They get a relatively full.
- Have mediocre Bible.
- An adequate Care Group Ministry.
- Support their preaching staff.
- Have a couple Gospel meetings or weekend seminars a year.

And they're satisfied.
On the other hand, a growth mentality is *constructively discontent.*
They are *never satisfied with status quo.* They are convinced that...

- the preaching can be engaging
- the worship can be more reverent and relevant
- the classes can be better taught
- the church can be more involved in the community

Those with a growth mentality are constantly looking ways to *improve.*

I think we can see this maintenance mentality at *Laodicea.* They were comfortable and saw no room for improvement. I certainly don't believe our church family is even remotely like Laodicea. But we must be careful not to have the same comfortable mind-set or one day we will be. Indeed, we must be *constructively discontent.*

Now I must point out here that a mentality is not *malcontent.* We must never be found thinking that everything should be done our way to be right. We must never be found constantly *griping and complaining* about...

- How things are done
- And what everyone else does wrong

Constructively discontent means able to *see the God* in what is going on...while *promoting and expecting* consistent improvement.

A maintenance mentality looks behind.

A growth mentality looks ahead.

Churches and church members in a maintenance mode *do a lot of reminiscing.*

- They think about the golden years when old brother so and so did the preaching.
- When they held Bible studies in their homes
- Went on campaigns and mission trips
- When they had an *intimate, forgiving, meaningful, mutual fellowship*
- They are constantly saying, "This is the way we used to do it." While a growth mentality learns from the past, it looks to the future.

I think Jesus encouraged this kind of mentality in Acts 1:8 when He told the apostles, "You shall be my witnesses both in Jerusalem, and in all Judea and Samaria, and even to the remotest part of the earth." How could eleven men ever expect to accomplish such a task? Only by walking by faith and trusting God for their future.

Then there's the church at Sardis in Revelation chapter 3. Sardis was living on a *reputation.* They were looking at the glory days in which they were *alive.* But when John told them they were *dead.*

Again, I'm not suggesting that we are like Sardis…neither do we want to be!

But, if we are not constituently vigilant, this mentality can creep in and we will be.

We must be visionary…looking ahead at what the future possibilities might become. Be ready for any and all doors that God might providentially open *to us…for us.*

*****

A maintenance mentality wants to stay the same.
A growth mentality wants edifying, meaningful change.

Here is something I want you to think about. We like to think that if we always do what we have always done, we will always get same results. While the truth is, if we always do what we have always done, we will always get *declining results.* Just because something worked once or twice or even for years, doesn't mean it will continue to work and work well.

We live in a changing world. Technology proves this to us every day. There comes a time to *let go of the old way of doing things.* And that time is when it *ceases* to produce the same result.

You see, if nothing ever changes, nothing ever grows. Farmers, cattlemen, gardeners, businessmen know this… And so do growing churches.

No…

- I'm *not* suggesting changing our *standard of authority.*
- I'm *not* talking about *unscriptural* change.

Second Timothy 3:16–17 tells us we must never change our standard of authority. All Scripture is God-breathed and is useful for teaching, rebuking, correcting, and training in righteousness so that the man of God may be thoroughly equipped for every good work.

You see, church, some things are *unscriptural*…and must *never* be changed. Some things are *nonscriptural.* Scripture just doesn't address the issue so *these can be changed.*

- Meeting times
- The order of services
- Songbooks or video projection

Are three examples of *nonscriptural* issue?

But within the authorization provided by scripture, we must be willing to change what should be changed. We must be willing to try new approaches...to try and apply new techniques. Here it is, church. Change for change's sake has no benefit, *but constructive change is beneficial.*

For instance, in the early part of the last century, the number one evangelistic tool was Gospel meeting. Nobody had anything else going on, so they would come to every service of a one...two...three times a week meeting, whether they were a member of the church or not.

Thousands have been converted this way. Perhaps you were one of them. But fifty to a hundred years later, we find it hard to even get our own members to make it out to such a series of meetings. Let alone get our neighbors to come. Should we doggedly hold on to this model? Thought-provoking questing.

A good biblical example of having to change can be found in Acts 19:8–9. Here, Luke tells us that Paul was preaching...*reasoning*...in the synagogue. But things reached a stand still. So what was no longer working, *Paul changed.* In fact, they were going backward because some were blaspheming the way. Paul changed the teaching place from the Jewish synagogue to the school of Tyrannus. And Scripture says that change... *All who lived in Asia heard the word of the Lord.*

A growth mentality is willing to accept scriptural change when change will produce growth, either spiritually or numerically.

*****

A maintenance mentality avoids problems.
A growth mentality faces them quickly.

Know this: Those who are maintenance minded try to *hide from problems* while the growth minded focus on solving them. Growth-minded leadership understands that ignored problems only get worse.

- Maintainers only think about the immediate fallout of a problem.
- Growers see the end result of dealing with the problem and doing so quickly.

This is biblically illustrated in Acts chapters 5 and 6.
The first problem was with Ananias and Sapphira.
Discipline was needed, and Peter addressed it *immediately*. What do you suppose would have happened if they had just over-looked this couple's sin because they were afraid others might leave the church? The sin of lying would have spread like leaven throughout the whole congregation. Granted they lost two members. But Acts 5:14 gives us the end result. *More and more men and women believed in the Lord and were added to their number.*
The second problem was with the Hellenistic widows.
They were being overlooked in the daily food distribution. Now, the apostles could have gotten worried about the possible fall-out over facing this issue of *racism* in the church. But instead they took immediate action and had the church appoint seven men to make sure everything was being taken care of property.
Again, the long-term result is found in Acts 6:7: "So the word of God spread. The number of disciples in Jerusalem increased rapidly, and a large number of priests became obedient to the faith."
Let me make a point.
I've often wondered, why did church leadership have to become involved in this problem? If every member of the Jerusalem church had the mind of Christ, the attitude, the heart of Jesus, and disposition of Christ, they would *not* have allowed the Grecian widows to go without food.
Church, we don't need the elders' permission to *go about doing good works*. We don't have to have leadership organize a program to

do what we ought to be doing ourselves...if we have the *attitude and behavior* of Christ... *Amen?*

Listen, if we see something that needs to be done...if it's reasonable and right, *do it...just do it!* And a godly eldership along with a scriptural working pastor will bless your attitude and behavior.

*****

A maintenance mentality focuses on members.
A growth mentality focuses on guests.

A maintaining congregation does not think about their *guests*. They often do not even try to make their guests feel *welcome*. They certainly don't make decisions about how the classes or the assemblies are to be conducted based on guests and their feelings and needs.

Paul addresses this issue in 1 Corinthians 14:23–25. So if the whole church comes together and everyone speaks in tongues, and inquirers or unbelievers comes in, they will say you are out of your mind? But if an unbeliever or inquirer comes in while everyone is teaching...*prophesying*...they are convinced of sin and are brought under judgment by all as the secrets of their hearts are laid bare. So they will fall down and worship God.

Our Bible classes and worship should be conducted in a way that our guests both *understand and are convinced and convicted by the Word. Amen?*

*****

A maintenance mentality kills a church.
A growth mentality maintains and grows it.

Churches are like trees. They are either growing or they are dying.

- When we are so intent on just trying to hang on to what we've already got, that we will *not* let go of what is no longer working, *we will not survive.*

- When we're so afraid of rocking the boat, trying to please everybody, that we will not condemn sin, *we'll flounder.*
- When we are so focused on pleasing ourselves that we will not do what is reasonable and right to *convince and convict* our guest, *we will die on the vine.*

I don't know a better way to make this point than to listen to Jesus from John chapter 15:

> I am the true vine, and my Father is the garden. He cuts off every branch in me that bears no fruit, while every branch that does bear fruit he prunes so that it will be even more fruitful. You are already clean because of the word I have spoken to you. Remain in me, and I will remain in you. No branch can bear fruit by itself; it must remain in the vine. Neither can you bear fruit unless you remain in me. I am the vine; you are the branches. If a man remains in me and I in him, he will bear much fruit; apart from me you can do nothing. If anyone does not remain in me, he is like a branch that is thrown away and withers; such branches are picked up, thrown into the fire and burned. If you remain in me and my words remain in you, ask whatever you wish, and it will be given you. This is to my Father's glory, that you bear much fruit, showing yourselves to be my disciples.

We note that most churches begin with a *growth mentality.* However, they usually progress to a point where they shift from wanting more growth to wanting to *protect the growth they already have.*

- Maybe they've finally become self-supporting and fear having to go back depending on outside support.

- Maybe they've built a building and fear not being able to make the payments.
- Maybe they've gained some wealthy members and fear losing them. Who knows? But it almost always happens.

We must not let that happens here. *We must keep the growth vision alive.* Remember, *attitude and expectation drive behavior.* So, when we plant, water, and cultivate, God promises to give the increase. *He promises growth. Amen?*

The challenge for us as a church and as individuals is to…

- *cultivate a growth mentality*
- and rid ourselves of simple *existing in a maintenance mode.*

And the world will be our oyster!

A Church Growth Model

Acts 2:36–47

If your church family is to grow, we must remove the *maintenance mentality* and replace it with a *growth mentality*...thinking *about* growth...planning *for* growth.

Most scholars and historians believe that by the Christian dispersion recorded in Acts chapters 8, the Jerusalem congregation could have grown to some twenty to thirty thousand souls.

- What caused such phenomenal growth from three thousand on Pentecost to possibly thirty thousand only a few years later?
- What are the *attitude and behavior* patterns of a growing church?

We need to hold up the first church, the Jerusalem church, as a model of congregation growth.

What does a Spirit-filled church look like?

Turn in your bibles to Acts chapter 2 and let's read our text together. Acts chapter 2... And I wait for you at the verse numbered 36...

> Therefore let all Israel be assured of this: God has made this JESUS, WHOM YOU CRUCIFIED, both Lord and Christ. When the people heard this,

they were cut to the heart and said to Peter and the other apostles, "Brother, what shall we do?" Peter replied, "Repent and be baptized, every one of you, in the name of Jesus Christ for the forgiveness of your sins. And you will receive the gift of the Holy Spirit. The promise is for you and your children and for all who are far off-for all whom the Lord our God will call." With many other words he warned them; and he pleaded with them, "Save yourselves from this corrupt generation." Those who accepted his message were baptized, and about three thousand were added to their number that day. They devoted themselves to the apostles' teaching and to the fellowship, to the breaking of bread and to prayer. Everyone was filled with awe, and many wonders and miraculous signs were done by the apostles. All the believers were together and had everything in common. Selling their possessions and goods, they gave to anyone as he had need. Every day they continued to meet together in the temple courts. They broke bread in their homes and ate together with glad and sincere hearts, praising God and enjoying the favor of all the people. And the Lord added to their number daily those were being saved.

*****

What we can learn from this passage about *church growth*...the marks of a growing church family.

First, they were a learning church.

Verse 42 says, "They devoted themselves to the apostles' teaching, and the fellowship, and the breaking of the bread, and the prayers."

The same plan laid out in this book was responsible for a church of around fifty to grow to over three hundred in just over three years. They quad-tripled their membership and offering. It does work if you work.

The Jerusalem congregation was a *studying* church…*a truth-seeking* church. Listen again, they *devoted* themselves to the apostles' doctrine.

These Spirit-filled converts were *not* enjoying some mystical experience which led them…

- to neglect their intellect,
- to despite theology,
- or to stop thinking.

On the contrary, they *devoted* themselves to God's Word…and *submitted* to its authority.

What's the application of this to us today?

- We must be a church that respects the Bible as God's will in our lives.
- We must be a community of believers that spends time studying.
- We must have Bible classes with teachers who will study, prepare, and present *interesting, thought-provoking, and motivational* lessons.
- A pulpit where truth is taught in such a loving manner that it will move us out of our comfort zone into *a more complete obedience to God.*
- As individuals, we must be willing to *accept and obey* truth wherever and whenever we find it.

It was Paul who admonished Timothy. *Study. Be diligent. To present yourself approved to God, a worker who does not need to be ashamed, rightly dividing the word of truth.*

Then one chapter later, Paul tells us why we are to be *diligent in our search and study of truth… Because all of Scripture is God-breathed and is useful for teaching, rebuking, correcting, and training in righteous-ness so that the man of God may be thoroughly equipped for every good work.*

So the first mark of a *Spirit-filled growing church* is that we be...

- a studying, truth-seeking church...
- that we be faithful to apostolic doctrine
- that we take seriously the authority of New Testament scripture
- and that we are willing to submit to it daily
- A growing church is one where...
- its ministers will expound the Bible from the pulpit
- its parents take personal responsibility of teaching their children from the Scriptures
- its members read and reflect upon the Word of truth every day
- we desire the sincere milk of the word that we may grow thereby

The Jerusalem church did *not* enjoy biblical growth until it become a *learning church. Amen?*

Secondly, Jerusalem was a loving, caring, and supportive church.

If the first mark is *study*, the second is *fellowship*. They devoted themselves to the apostles' teaching and to *fellowship*.

It was the apostle John who wrote, "*Our fellowship* is with the Father and with his Son Jesus Christ." It was Paul who added the phrase "*the fellowship* of the Spirit.*"

So authentic *fellowship* is *trinitarian*. It's our common *participation* in the *love, grace*, and *mercy* of God. We come from different backgrounds, nations, and cultures, but we are *unified* by our common relationship as children of God.

So it's on these two ideas that Luke lays his emphasis in our text. Note that verse 44 (emphasis added) says, "All the believers were together and they had all things in common, Selling their possessions and goods they *gave* to anyone as he need."

This verse has been disturbing to some. It's the kind of verse we jump over rather quickly in our hurry to get to the next verse, thus avoiding its challenge. What does it mean? Does it mean that we should all sell everything we own and give the proceeds to the poor?

Perhaps this verse is meant to be understood in the context of what Jesus said in Luke 12:15 (emphasis added): "Life does *not* consist in the abundance of our possessions."

Jesus is telling us that there are more important things in life than what we own. You see, the absolute *prohibition* of private property is Marxist, *not* Christian. The sin of Ananias and Sapphire was lying. It was *not* that they were keeping back part of the proceeds from the sale of their property.

It was Peter who queried, "Before you sold your property was it now your own? And after you sold it…were not the funds at your disposal?"

Not everybody in Jerusalem sold and gave away everything. We read in verse 46 that they met in one another's homes. *They hadn't sold them!* The giving and selling were both voluntary. Growing churches cannot avoid the challenge of these verses…to love and care for one another in the family. Why should this surprise us…*the fruit of the Spirit is love?*

This first church loved and cared for one another enough to not only share in God's *grace* blessing but they were willing to share their *possessions* with those less fortunate.

This becomes even more evident in Acts 6 where seven men were appointed to serve the Grecian widows.

You see, *growing churches have a tender social conscience.* Not because we think we can solve the economic problems of the world but because the New Testament calls us to a *simplistic, content, and generous lifestyle.*

If our God is a generous God, we must be generous too.

*****

Jerusalem was a worshiping church.

Note our verse. *They devoted themselves to* the *breaking of the bread and prayers.* Luke uses the *definite article. The* breaking of die bread is evidently the Lord's Supper…and possibly a fellowship meal

46

as well like at Passover. After all, this was the pattern Jesus used in the Last Supper. Both phrases refer to Christian *worship*.

What impresses me about the worship of the early church is its balance in two respects...*formal and informal.*

It was both formal and informal...in the temple *and in their* homes.

They continued to attend the prayer services at the temple. This is indicated by Peter and John in verse 1 of Acts 3. I'm sure they went there wanting to reform the Jewish temple worshipers to a clearer understanding of Jesus and His once-for-all sacrificial offering for their sins, but they *did* continue in these prayer services, which had a degree of formality.

Secondly, they supplemented these services with their own *simple, informal, unstructured, and spontaneous* meetings at home.

Indeed, growing churches have *formal worship services.* And they have *informal meetings* in one another's homes. We may call them care groups or fellowship groups or fun food fellowship groups or Bible studies or no name at all...just informal household gatherings. You see, we need the experience of both just as they did in the early church.

No wonder the Hebrews writer admonishes us not to forsake such assemblies—both formal and informal. Jewish Tabernacle and temple worship was a daily affair...and so should our Christian worship be.

This is one of the premises behind Wednesday evening gatherings.

Wednesday evening services are no more than a human effort devised to support our need to *worship God and be strengthened* daily *by a common fellowship.*

Church growth, both spiritually and numerically, is tied not just to formal Sunday morning services *but daily,* including Sunday and Wednesday evening opportunities to worship and praise God.

I never understood those who believe themselves to be doctrinally correct but who failed to *take advantage* of such worship opportunities.

Next, we see that the Jerusalem church was joyous fellowship.

Note *with* glad and sincere *hearts.*

Luke uses a word that means "exaltation." They were not just joyous... They had an *exalted* form of joy.

- God sent his Son into the world.
- He had sent his Spirit into their hearts.

How could they not be joyful over the mighty acts of God in their lives?

And the fruit of the Spirit is *what? Love... Joy... Peace.* This scripture is telling us where the Holy Spirit is, joy should be there also.

Our *church services* and our *informal fellowship events* should be filled with joy.

Have you ever gone to church service where...

- everybody is dressed in black,
- nobody smiles,
- nobody laughs,
- nobody talks,
- the hymns are at a snail's pace?

That's a funeral!

Christianity is a *joyful* religion, and we need to have a note of *joy* in our services.

Indeed, they are to be *reverent.*

Verse 43 notes that *fear, awe,* and *wonder* came upon every soul. When we read these together, we understand that we can be *joyously reverent* in our worship and in our formal gatherings.

Then number five, the Jerusalem church was evangelistic.

Churches must not become ingrown toenails...self-regarding... self-satisfying.

- There is a world to be won for Christ.
- We must be concerned for the lost.
- We must not be so absorbed with ourselves that we have no mission outreach.

Evangelism was a focus of this church... We know this from Acts 8.

You see, when one goes to Acts chapter 8, we find the Christians were scattered all over the Jewish world by governmental persecution.

Listen as we read verses 1 and 4: "A great persecution broke out against the church at Jerusalem, and all except the apostles were scattered throughout Judea and Samaria... Those who had been scattered preached the word wherever they went."

Did God have to bring about this event so that His children would carry the good news to others outside the environs of Jerusalem? Sobering question.

God help us to grow the church where we are and be willing to submit to Jesus's commands. *Into all the world, preach to all creation.*

Well, I want you to notice the last sentence in the text: "And the Lord added to their number." Our KJ Bible says, "To the church... Daily those who were being saved."

Two things here...

One, only the lord can add a person to the church, not the preacher, not by a vote of the church family...only by faith, repentance, and baptism.

This is the biblical pattern. The three thousand believed in Jesus, repented of their sins, and were baptized for the remission of their sins and the gift of the Holy Spirit.

Secondly, those added were those being saved.

This tells us that God didn't save them *without adding them to the church*. And he didn't add them to the church *without saving them*. Salvation and membership in God's family...His number... always belong together. The two are inseparable. If I understand this verse correctly, there are no such things as *unhooked Christians*. No such thing as what is known today as *nones*, Christians without any church affiliation

What about you and your preacher, are you interested in church growth? Are they really?

Are we saved? Has God added us to His number? Are we a part of God's church family?

Some things the church leadership can do to help the congregation to "grow the church." Call a meeting after services and select several members to head up five or six members to do the following. First group to go to all the members who have left the church, for whatever reason, and not just one visit but as many as it takes to get them to come back, and this has to be done with nothing but love and not just duty. These people that have left the church will be able to tell if you are sincere and really want them back, and if you are not completely sincere and loving, you will lose them forever. This first group is probably the most important group of all, so fill it with the most loving, kind, and sincere people you have. Groups 2 through whatever (5 or 6) or more and give them all tracts to carry with them and not just on one occasion but always have these tracts with them all the time. A recent study shows that 70 percent of all new souls won were done before they ever got to church by individuals that talked to them outside of the church and convinced them to attend. Start these groups out by walking from the church in four different directions. There is most likely enough people within walking distance of your church to fill it up more than double. Just have to talk to them and bring them with you, and then spread out from there. Malls, school, on the street, stores where you shop, this can be limitless.

Have one group watch the local newspaper and every time anyone is admitted to the hospital, have someone visit with a card and say a prayer and let them know that you genuinely care and invite them to church. This should be done on a daily or at least a weekly basis. Every time there is a wedding announcement, make sure you send the newlyweds a card and go see them, inviting them to church. When there is an award to someone in the paper, send them or visit them with a card or tract. When there is a death, always visit with a card and let the ones that are left know that they are loved and that they are invited to church.

But above all, this has to be done with the right spirit and with love, or it will all be in vain. Leave the phone number of the church or preacher and let everyone know that you will be back and check on them. That they are important and you will continue your visits, with their permission, of course.

Try it, this works alone with everything else in this book. I know it works because I helped a church grow from around fifty members to close to three hundred in less than three years; however, it will only work if everyone puts the required effort into making it work. *Everyone.* Just imagine all the souls that could be won. Wouldn't be hard to double or triple the membership. The first commandment when the Church was established on the Day of Pentecost was to go and preach the Gospel to every living creature. All you have to do is in your own community.

13

Wanted: Good Soil

In Mark 4:3–9, Jesus taught the crowd using the parable of the sower. After this, his disciples asked him about the meaning and Jesus explained the parable to them.

> The sower sows the word. And these are the ones along the way where the word is sown: when they hear, Satan immediately comes and takes away the word that is sown in them. And these are the ones sown on rocky ground: the ones who. when they hear the word, immediately receive it with joy. And they have no root in themselves, but endure for a while; then, when tribulation or persecution arises on account of the word. immediately they fall away. And others are the ones sown among thorns. They are those who hear the word, but the cares of the world and the deceitfulness of riches and the desires for other things enter in and choke the word, and it proves unfruitful. But those that were sown on the good soil are the ones who hear the word and accept it and bear fruit, thirtyfold and sixtyfold and a hundredfold. (Mark 4:14–20 ESV)

There are several things that this parable can teach us. For those of us who have been Christians for a long time, this is well-traveled ground. We have probably heard multiple lessons on the various types of soil Jesus mentioned and the responsibility we have as followers of Jesus to sow the seed. I hope that as you read this again, you take an honest look at yourselves and determine which of these soil types best describe us. I don't think that there is anyone who reads this that does not want to be counted as the *good soil*. I also believe that God would like for all people to be *good soil*. So, if people want to be good soil and God wants us to be good soil, then why aren't we all good soil?

What does it take to be good soil? Jesus gives the answer in Mark 4:23–24 (ESV): "'If anyone has ears to hear, let him hear.' And he said to them, 'Pay attention to what you hear: With the measure you use, it will be measured to you, and still more will be added to you.'"

The first thing we see is that we must be willing to listen to what Jesus has to say. Being willing to listen is a demonstration of humility. It puts us in the position of learners. When we think we know best, that there is nothing we can learn, we resist listening. This happens in our personal relationships, doesn't it? We resist listening to others because we believe we know better and we want to do things our own way. The first step to becoming the good soil is to humble ourselves and listen to Jesus.

The second thing is that we not only listen to Jesus but also put into practice the things He says. We pay attention to Him and follow as He directs. The disciples didn't understand the parable at first, but they moved closer to Jesus to learn the meaning. There seems to be many things that the disciples didn't immediately understand, but the more they listened and followed Jesus, the better soil they became.

When we stop and think about it, learning from Jesus and continually following Him seem to be the correctives needed to move from the bad soil to the good.

Humbling ourselves and recognizing our need and His love have a tendency to soften our hearts. The more time we spend with Jesus, the deeper our faith in him grows. The more we pay attention to Jesus, the more we see what is truly important in our lives and enables us to prioritize our lives as he wants. God wants good soil. We want to be good soil. Are we willing to listen and follow? Are we willing to let him work on us so that we may become good soil and bear fruit for the kingdom?

Spectator vs Ministry

Christianity is not a spectator sport. Religion, our relationship with God, is not based upon our attending worship services. It has much more to do with what is going on in our heart. Jesus came to take the law of Moses out of the physical and place religion in your heart. Hate became mental murder, and lust became mental adultery. He was the One who said it is out of the heart that the mouth speaks. Life behaviors come from the heart, both good and bad. It's easy to attend a worship service once a week, even three times a week. It's quite another thing to purify the heart, become God's temple, His instrument of righteousness, His living sacrifice, a living stone in His spiritual house, a royal priest, a holy person who belongs to God because we are doing God's work. Church, we're not God's person just because we gather on Sunday morning. Our relationship with God, our righteousness, is seen in service! We're better Bible students than to think that Christian duty is bound up in attendance, being a spectator. We must become participants in His kingdom work, in kingdom responsibility. Jesus pictured the kingdom of God as a place of work—a field, a vineyard, a merchant, a Steward, a landlord, etc. Our relationship with Him is found in our finding our purpose, gift, blessing, talent, responsibility; it's found in finding our place and putting ourselves to work in His kingdom—ministry!

When we stand in judgment, God is not going to ask how many church services we attended, but what we did in His kingdom. The church needs additional deacons, teachers, van drivers, those who will visit the sick, shut-ins, and the elderly, lonely, and needy. Grab a ministry sheet and count the areas of work listed, what are we thinking? When Jesus paints a picture of judgment, it's not about being a spectator but about serving the Jesus in others. So the question becomes, why aren't we involved in His service? What keeps from finding our place and purpose in His kingdom?

Perhaps it's a lack of commitment. At Mount Sinai, it was "*No other gods before Me.*" From Jesus: "Love God with all your heart, mind, strength and soul." Commitment is giving God His rightful place in our lives. For most of us, we made a decision for Jesus years ago, but have we made a commitment? Marriage is a commitment. We made a decision to get married, but the real success in a marriage is based upon commitment. If there is no commitment with our decision, divorce becomes a reality. A pilot going down the runway must make a commitment to fly. As a plane gains speed, there comes an invisible line that, when crossed, the pilot must commit to take off. At that point, the speed of the aircraft is too fast to abort; if he does, a crash is imminent. Question! Have we made a decision or a commitment? Ministry is a commitment! Are we a spectator minister?

A focus on self. We live in a "it's about me" culture, narcissism rules! Life is not about us but about our becoming like Jesus. His agenda must become our agenda. "'This is how we know we are in Him: Whoever claims to live in Him must walk as Jesus walked.' Jesus said: 'Anyone who will not... Follow me cannot be my disciple.'" The statement of Jesus on genuine discipleship contains only three words: "*Come follow me.*" Discipleship is about walking as Jesus walked, following in His footsteps. Opportunities to become like Jesus are found in ministry, not in attendance. Don't pass that invisible line where our relationship with Jesus crashes because we would not serve. Got to ask, are we a spectator or minister?

Our western world thinking. We have a western world mind-set, which is not always a good thing. Westerners don't serve, we rule. Servants are seen as humble beings; rulers are kings! We want to be in charge. We're not content until we become the CEO. But it was Jesus who said, "*The greatest among you is he who serves.*" Church, we must let go of our pride, our western mentality, and become servants. Think on these scriptures: "The Lord takes delight in His people; He crowns the humble with salvation" (Ps. 149:4). James says, "God opposes the proud but give grace to the humble... Humble yourselves before Lord, and he will lift you up." Let's be willing to wrap Jesus towel of service about our waist and wash feet. Abundant foot washing opportunities are found all about us. Do we have a towel? Are we ministers or spectators?

We don't see God in our opportunities. I think I can remember a time in the church when we believed that God didn't still work in the lives of His people, equipping them for ministry. Here's truth: "His power is at work in us" (Eph. 3:21). The Hebrews' writer says, "God will equip us with all we need to do His will" (Heb. 13:21). Paul says, "Be confident of this that He who began a good work in you will carry it on to completion" (Phil. 1:6). Indeed, God is at work in us! God is working through His ministry system to provide us with opportunities, not to just attend services but to serve. Will we become spectators or ministers?

May God bless our thoughts on this challenge, and may He bless our decisions to serve.

Are We a Fan, Follower, or Pharisee?

Luke 9:23–26, 51–62; Mark 10:17–22

As we read through the Gospels, we'll find example after example where Jesus puts people in a position where they *must choose. Fan? Follower? Or Pharisee?*

The first thing has to do with serving Jesus only when it's *convenient* and *comfortable.*

Verse 57 states, "As they were walking along the road, a man said to him… I will follow you wherever you go."

He was saying, I will follow you without reservation. Then Jesus gives him the facts about genuine discipleship. *Foxes have holes and birds of the air have nests, but the* son of man *has no place to lay his head.*

Jesus must have known that this man loved *comfort* and *convenience* more than following him.

Maybe that's what's keeping us from becoming a *follower.*

- Jesus didn't come to this earth so that we could be comfortable.
- Jesus didn't come into the world to meet our felt needs.
- He didn't come into the world to tweak our personality.
- He didn't come to fine-tune our manners and smooth out our rough spots.

He came to totally transform us! Change us! Remold, reshape, and remake us!

And if we think this is an *easy, convenient, and comfortable task,* we're on a collision course with Jesus.

The objective of the Gospel is not to make us a well-balanced, well-behaved person but to turn our life upside down. *To change us completely!* When we quit fighting for controls of our life, surrender *everything to Him.* When we die to self-*daily* and live for him, we'll find life that's truly life.

Only then do we become a *follower...* not a fan.

A preacher tells a story about hearing that a man was leaving their church because of the way he preached... So he calls him, saying, I understand you're leaving our church because you don't like my sermons. The man launched into a rambling explanation. But somewhere in his lengthy explanation, he said, "Well, whenever I listen to one of the messages, I feel like you're trying to *interfere with my life."*

Indeed, Jesus came to interfere with our lifestyle!

This man was saying, I want to follow Jesus...

- But don't ask me to forgive the person who has offended me.
- Don't ask me to release that bitterness and resentment because I'm not gonna go there.
- I want to follow Jesus but don't ask me to give up my weekends.
- Don't ask me to set aside a sum from my wages each Lord's day.
- I want to follow Jesus but you have no right to demand I be ethical in my business dealings. A man's got to do what a man's got to do to get ahead today.
- I'll follow Jesus but don't talk to me about my sex life. I can't help my desires.
- I want to follow Jesus but don't talk to me about *total and absolute* commitment.

You see, fans go to church to be *entertained or to experience the rituals.*

The rituals make them feel religious… But rituals don't make a difference in how we live. *Rituals don't change lives.*

Followers go to church to…

- experience Jesus
- hear Jesus
- see Jesus
- touch Jesus
- remember Jesus

You see, experiencing Jesus…

- changes us
- disciplines us
- shapes
- remolds
- and remakes us into *a different person.*

Here it is: we should leave these services *looking more like Jesus* than when we came… Not because of form or ritual but because we have *experienced* Jesus.

A man once told me, speaking of his prodigal daughter… We raised her in church. But we didn't raise her *in Christ.* She grew up learning to be a *fan* instead of a *follower* of Jesus.

Most parents want their kids to have a little bit of God. They want their kids to have some biblical morals. But it's most dangerous to be raised with *a little bit of Jesus.* It's like an inoculation. A little bit can make one immune to the real thing.

Our second fan is found in verses 59 and 60. He is filled with good intentions, *but* procrastination *rules his life.*

Jesus invites… Follow me… The man replied, "Lord, first let me go and bury my father." Jesus said to him, "Let the dead bury their own dead, but you go and proclaim the kingdom of God."

Maybe we hear this man's excuse for putting Jesus off, thinking that Jesus is being a little too *hardcore.* I mean, come on, let the guy go bury his dad!

There are some things we don't know. Was his dad terminally ill? Was he sick at all?

He may have been saying. Jesus…

- I'll follow you when my parents die.
- When I get my inheritance.
- When they can no longer disapprove.

Then I will follow you.

Again, this man's intentions appear to be good. But Jesus *sees the heart*. Only God knows whether or not we really *intended to carry through* with our good intentions.

What we do know is, one of the first words out the guy's mouth is…*first.*

The first thing he does is put Jesus off. "I want to follow you. I really do…but right now."

Remember the man I've told you about? We raised our kids together, bought and sold cattle together, laughed and cried, buried our parents together. One night we talked about Jesus *all night long*. And as the sun rose over the breakfast table, he promised me he *intended* to become a Christian *one day…someday!*

Well, that was almost forty years ago, and today, *this morning*, he is terminally ill and has only a few days to live. And it's too late… much too late.

Sometimes…

- We're found treating our relationship with Jesus like the diet we mean to start…*tomorrow.*
- We put off involving ourselves in ministry like we put off going to the gym. We have *good intentions*. But do our good intentions make any significant difference? *No!* Not really… Not if we keep *procrastinating.*

Procrastination robs us of life.
Remember the reading in Ecclesiastes.
First I was dying to *finish high school and start college.*

Then I was dying to *finish college and start a career.*
Then I was dying to *marry and have children.*
Then I was dying for our children to *grow up and leave the home.*
Then I was dying to *retire.*
And now… *I'm dying!*
And suddenly I realize *I forgot to live!*
Is this us? Will we put Jesus off until it is *too late?*
This man's excuse wasn't enough for Jesus.

- What's holding us back from becoming a follower rather than just being a fan?
- What's keeping us from a deeper, more intimate relationship with God?
- What's keeping us from saying yes to some ministry that the Holy Spirit is inviting us into?

Yes, like this man, it may seem to us that our excuse is very legitimate, *but is it? Is it?*

All the while, Jesus is saying the time is *now. Today is the day of salvation.*

Will we become a fan or follower?

Verse 61 states, "Discipleship is about priority and commitment."

I will follow you, Lord, but first let me go back say goodbye to my family. Jesus replied, "No one who puts his hard to the plow and looks back is fit for service in the kingdom of God."

Here it is, church. Jesus isn't looking for *half-hearted* followers.

Following Him part-time isn't an option.

Is Jesus one-of-many…*or is He our one and only?*

Fans want to make Jesus me-of-many.

Followers are to make Him their *one and only.*

Let's pretend you walk into a New Orleans restaurant and see me sitting at a table having a candlelight dinner with another woman. You come up and ask who the woman is and what I am doing. I say that I am on a date, and you a say "What about your wife?" I respond by saying, "Oh, well, I still love her too. But this isn't our date night... Our date night is on Thursday. I can date who I want the rest of the week."

You walk away angry and disgusted. You decide that someone needs to tell his wife. So you call her and tell her. Well, imagine that I come home from my date. You've already told wife. She meets me at door and says, "Hi, honey, did you have a nice time with your date?"

Now this story is really getting fictional!

You don't have to know your wife to know that her reaction would be *jealous anger.*

God is a jealous God. He wants to be *first and foremost* in our life. Jesus is clear that God must reign over every arena of life.

- *No others gods before me.*
- *Seek* first *the kingdom of God and his righteousness.*
- *Love the lord with* all *your hurt,* all *soul,* all *mind, and* all *your strength.*

Do we hear *commitment and priority* in these verses?

God wants top drawer...top shelf...first place status.

He doesn't want our one-day-a-week affection. *He wants our whole being.*

Jesus makes it plain in Revelation 3:16 that He's not satisfied with *lukewarm* discipleship.

Jesus wants a relationship that has priority and commitment. Are we willing? *As we* leave Luke 9 to find our next fan... One that's familiar to all... The Rich Young Ruler in Mark 10.

> As Jesus started on his way, a man ran up to him and fell on his knees before him. "Good teacher," he asked, "what must I to inherit eternal life?" "Why do call me good?" Jesus answered. "No-one is good—except God alone. You know the commandments: Do not murder, do not commit adultery. do not steal. do give false testimony. do not defraud, honor your father and mother.'" "Teacher," he declared. "all these I have

kept since I was a boy." Jesus looked at him and loved him. "One thing you lack," he said. "Go. sell everything you have and give to the poor, and you will have treasure in heaven. Then come. follow me" At this the man's face fell. He went away sad, because he had great wealth.

Here it is, church. Fans place *money—material things—*before Jesus. Regardless of who we are, how *little or much* we have, there'll come a time when *all* our money and possessions will be meaningless.

All that will matter is, *are we a fan or a follower? Are we?*

There were those in Jesus's day who made no pretense about being a fan or follower.

The Pharisees were dead set against Jesus. And the reason was that He set Himself up against their religious traditions.

They were religious. But they were religiously wrong. And here's the problem: *they had* no intention *of changing.* It's one thing to be religiously wrong. It's something else to have no intention of changing.

You see, the Pharisees held *tradition* more important than *truth.*

- When John the Baptist came preaching *truth*, Scripture says all Judea came to be baptized. They displayed a *willingness to change.*
- Three thousand on Pentecost were willing to shed tradition for truth.
- When Peter and Cornelius recognized truth, they left tradition behind.
- When Aquila and Priscilla taught Apollos the truth, he let go of tradition and became a follower.

Jesus was not at odds with the Pharisees because they were *not* keeping the law of Moses… Because they were…even to the letter, but because they held tradition above God's truth.

Got to ask the question, are we standing on *tradition?* Or upon *truth? God's truth? The Holy Inerrant Text?*

I sincerely hope we are, *but if not…but if not,* we must know that it's truth that…

- *sanctifies us,*
- *sets us free from sin, and*
- *saves us.*

It's obedience to truth that determines whether or not we become *a fan or a follower.*

Well, the invitation hasn't changed.

Jesus still says, *"If anyone would come after me, he must deny himself, take up his cross and follow me… Be like me… Conform to my image."*

The key word in Jesus's invitation is *anyone.*

- No matter what our story…
- No matter what we've done…
- No matter the ugliness…
- Or how repulsive our sin…

Jesus invites us *to be forgiven* by becoming a child of God through faith, repentance, and New Testament baptism…immersed in water for the forgiveness of sins.

Anyone includes those of us who are followers But have *fallen… stumbled…have become more of a fan than follower.* Jesus invites us to come home. Make things right with God.

Anyone is an all-inclusive term.

- Anyone means everyone.
- Anyone means me and you.

16

Soul Shepherding

Philippians 2:5

There can be no doubt that God desires we each be conformed to the image of His Son, that we have a Jesus heart, attitude, disposition, and behavior, and that we be like Him. This is especially true of leaders in the church of Jesus Christ. Angry reactions, lustful impulses, conflict avoidance, emotional distance, prideful self-reliance, materialism, apathy, power plays, and inability to work well with others sabotage godly intentions that lead to failure. Like Paul, we must be aware of our weaknesses and work to eliminate them.

> I find this law at work: When I want to do good, evil is right there with me. For in my inner being I delight in God's law; but I see another law at work in my body, waging war against the law of my mind and making me a prisoner of the law of sin at work within. What a wretched man that makes me! Who will rescue me from this body of death? Thanks be to God—through Jesus Christ our Lord. (Rom. 7:21–25)

Emotional immaturity undermines our influence for Christ. This is true for preachers, elders, parents, and people of the pew—even those who are highly gifted, wealthy, or famous. This is even true for leaders who are deeply committed to Christ and earnest about loving other people—because neglecting our emotions…

- weakens our ability to hear the Lord's voice,
- weakens our ability to experience His presence, and
- weakens our acting, walking "in step with His Spirit."

Listen, church, when we see someone walking outside the truth, going in the wrong direction, we have an obligation to shepherd that soul. "Keep watch over yourselves all the flock of which the Holy Spirit has made you overseers. Be shepherds of the church of God, which He bought with His own blood… So be on your guard!" (Acts 20:28–31). I'm aware that this admonition was given to the Ephesians elders, but many other Scripture can be given affirming the fact that this also a responsibility of any and every child of God. Aren't we to watch over ourselves, our brothers and sisters, the straying, the false teachers, and others that would lead the church astray of God's will and word? Of course!

Here it is, church, spiritual leadership is a lot deeper than believing and doing what's right—the Lord looks at the heart. He wants our heart to be right, motive to be right. Samuel was preparing to anoint a new king for Israel, a leader of God's people, His family, and church. "Do not consider his appearance or his height, for I have rejected him. The Lord does not look at the things man looks at. Man looks at the outward appearance, but the Lord looks at the heart" (1 Sam. 16:7). When church leaders lack right and pure motives, when they ignore their weaknesses, they are likely to hurt people, even whole church communities. "Search me out, O God, know my heart. Shine your light on my anxious feelings and thoughts. Show me if any of my ways are hurtful or sinful; lead me in your way of life" (Ps. 139:23–24; paraphrased).

Loving, Caring, Serving, and Restoring

Even though we're a mixture of people with different personalities, different backgrounds, from different parts of the country, with different ideas, different convictions, different faults, different needs, we're family! And we enjoy being together because we have a common faith in God and love for Jesus. A love that transforms us into being like Him, loving and caring for one another, and others!

Here is something else we have in common: we all fail! At one time or another, all of us find ourselves in need of someone who will become our helper, healer, restorer, someone who will come along side us, pick us up, dust us off, mend our wounds, carry our burdens, nurse us back to spiritual health.

Well, loving, caring, serving one another is as old as time itself. It was Cain who asked in Genesis chapter 4, "Am I my brother's keeper." The answer was evident before God. Yes! Yes! Nothing. Nothing becomes plainer than the fact that as God's children, we are to look out for one another.

- Proverbs 17:17 reads, "A friend loves at all times, a brother is born for adversity."
- Matthew 22:37–38 has Jesus saying we are to "love God with all our heart, mind, body and soul. And to love our neighbor as ourselves."
- Matthew 7:12 says we are to "treat others, as we would have them treat us."

- Philippians 2:4 has Paul insisting we "place the interest of others before our own."

This is not a suggestion—it's a command! We are to be like Jesus, consider others before ourselves. Our attitude must be like that of Jesus. He did not consider equality with God as something to hold on to but emptied himself...taking on the very nature of a servant.

> Brothers, if someone is caught in a sin. you who are spiritual should restore him gently. But watch yourself. or you also may be tempted. Carry each other's burdens, and in this way you will fulfill the law of Christ. If anyone thinks he is something when he is nothing, he deceives himself. Each one should test his own actions. Then he can take pride in himself, without comparing himself to somebody else, for each one should carry his own load Let us not become weary in doing, for at the proper time we will reap a harvest if we do not give up. Therefore. we have opportunity, let us do good to all people, especially to those belong to the family of believers. (Gal. 6:1–5, 9–10)

See what we can learn about loving, caring, serving, and restoring one another.

First, we must be spiritual. *"You who are spiritual should restore him."* Paul didn't say we must be perfect. Spirituality must not be equated with perfection. The spirituality that Paul speaks of can be found in the last verses of the previous chapter: "The fruit of the Spirit is love, joy, peace, patience, kindness, goodness, faithfulness, gentleness and self-control." No! We may not possess all the fruit of the Spirit all the time. None of us has been completely transformed into the image of His Son. But we are working at it. This is spirituality, our being formed into the image of Jesus. It is a present and an ongoing event.

Secondly, we must be humble. Paul says each of us, as restorers, must watch ourselves, lest we also be tempted. We are all susceptible! Paul says, "Watch how you see yourself." We must not think ourselves to be something special. "Do not think of yourselves more highly then you ought" (Rom. 12:3). A restorer can't be self-righteous. We must be people of humility. When a brother senses one's self-righteous attitude, they just naturally shrink back, unwilling to accept our help, encouragement, or direction.

We must be gentle. "You who are spiritual should restore him gently." There's no place for a mean, harsh spirit in restoration work. If we have a mean spirit, if we are always finding fault with others, if we are critical and judgmental of others, if we are listening to and passing on gossip, and if we have a loose tongue, we have no place as a restorer. It was said of Jesus that "a bruised reed He would not break, a smoldering wick He would not snuff out." *Hardball is out.* Gentleness is in.

We are to be persistent. *"Let us not become weary in doing good."* Let us not give up this work of bringing souls back into an intimate relationship with their Father God and His people. Why? "For we will reap if we faint not." There is a blessing for those who will love, care, and serve the Jesus in others. "Therefore, as we have opportunity, let us do good to all people, especially to those who belong to the family of believers."

I know there are some of you who are trying to help restore someone right now. And I know you are tired: tired of being used. Tired of their excuses. Tired of the manipulation. Tired of trying and trying and trying. But we must be like our Father God, never, never gives up. If we could get those that have left or wandered away from the church to come back, the church wouldn't be able to hold all of them. We need to train people to actively work on these people and to not give up.

Allow me to end with a neat story about how each of us should behave toward one another.

A marine walked into the ICU. A nurse met him at the door saying, "Your father has had a serious heart event and could die at any moment." The marine stood in the room for a moment surveying the situation and took the dying man's hand. There were mutual squeezes in affirmation of love and presence.

Through the night, the nurse encouraged the soldier to leave: get something to eat or drink. He never left and continued to hold the old man's hand. At morning's first light, the nurse hurries into the room saying, "Your father has passed."

Releasing the man's hand, the marine said, "Who is this man?" The nurse was startled. "Why, he's your father!"

"Not my father. I've never seen this man before in my life."

The nurse said, "Well, why didn't you tell me?"

The marine replied, "As I entered the room, I assessed the situation and saw the need. This man needed a son. He was much too sick to know who I was. Knowing how much he needed me, I stayed."

Wow! I got to tell you, folk, this is what loving, caring, and serving others is all about! Seeing the need and serving! Seeing the need and staying. "As oft as you do it to the least of these, you do it to me."

18

We Have to Rise above Complacency

Revelation 3:14–2

Revelation chapters 2 and 3 have Jesus addressing the seven churches of Asia. The ancient world saw the number seven as a *perfect number,* representing absolute *completeness.* Jesus instructing John to write to *seven churches* appears to a complete representation of the *total* brotherhood of believers with its *weakness and strong points.*

So the weaknesses and maturity we see in the second-century church represent *our weaknesses and strengths also. It's as if these letters were written to us.*

Let's see what we can learn from this *letter to the Laodiceans.*

Join me in Revelation chapter 3. We begin our reading together with the verse numbered 14:

> To the angel of the church in Laodicea write:
> These are the words of the Amen, the faithful and true witness, the ruler of God's creation. I know your deeds, that you are neither cold nor hot. I wish you were either one or the other! So, because you are lukewarm—neither hot nor cold—I am about to spit you out of my mouth. You say, I am rich; I have acquired wealth and do not need a thing. But you do not realize that you are wretched, pitiful, poor, blind and naked.

I counsel you to buy from me gold refined in the fire, so that you can become rich; and white clothes to wear, so that you can cover your shameful nakedness; and salve to put on your eyes, so that you can see. Those whom I love I rebuke and discipline. So be earnest, and repent. Here I am! I stand at the door and knock If anyone hears my voice and opens the door. I will come in and eat with him, and he with me. To him who overcomes. I will give the right to sit with me on my throne, just as I overcame and sat down with my Father on his throne. He Who has an ear, let him hear what the Spirit says to the churches.

*****

A pulpit talk on church growth...
What it takes to become the church we all want.
Come, let's see what we can learn from the lips of Jesus.

In Colossians 4:15–16
First, we must understand that Jesus knows what we need.
The opening words of verse 15: "I know your deeds."
Jesus knows the church. He knows us.

- Jesus knows *everything* about us
- The best and the worst...
- He knows the trials we're facing
- He knows what we are *thinking*
- Our *motives*
- He knows where we're failing and ways in which we're improving
- We might hide our thinking and motives from others, but we *hide nothing* from Him

What an awesome thought! *Jesus knows!*

Jesus knows us *individually*. He knows us as *a church family.*

Individually and corporately, the Laodicean church had been bitten by the bug of complacency.

The problem was a lack of zeal and fervor for the Lord and His kingdom work. Verses 15–16 (emphasis added) states, "I know your deeds. that you are neither cold nor hot. I wish you were either one or the other! So, because you're *lukewarm—neither hot nor cold*—I am about to spit you out my mouth."

Even though the water in Laodicea was good at the source, by the time it got to the city, *it was both dirty and lukewarm…with a foul sickening taste.* Visitors would often be seen spitting it out.

You see…

- some churches make the Lord *weep,*
- some make the Lord *angry, but*
- Laodicea made Jesus *sick.*

It was John R. W. Stott who wrote, "The Laodicean church was spiritually *half-hearted.*" Perhaps none of the seven churches is more appropriate to our culture than this one. It describes vividly the *respectable, sentimental, nominal, skin-deep, and complacent* religiosity which is so widespread among us today.

Indeed, the Laodicean church was *politically correct* but was *sickening* to Jesus. They had lost their *zeal and fervor…* their *excitement…* for the Lord and His work. It was Paul who wrote, "*Never be lacking in zeal.* But keep your spiritual *fervor* serving the Lord."

Jesus was *not* saying, I wish that you were either spiritually *hot* or spiritually *cold*, as in…

- with Me or against Me
- dead or alive
- enthusiastic or apathetic
- anemic or strong

He is saying…

- I wish you were like the water in Hierapolis—therapeutic and healing…
- Or like the water in Colossi—*refreshing, invigorating, thirst-quenching, clear and pure, motivated*…but because you are *neither one…just lukewarm.* It sickens me.

Jesus is saying to Laodicea and to us this I can't tolerate fence riding *neutrality.*

People, nothing…not one thing…inhibits a church's growth any more than a *neutral, apathetic, indifferent, careless* attitude and behavior on the part of its membership.

The second problem Jesus address in this church is their self-sufficiency. Read verses 17–18 (emphasis added) with me:

> You say, 'I am rich; I have acquired wealth and… *Listen now… Do not need a thing.*' But you do not realize that you are wretched, pitiful, poor, blind and naked. I counsel you to buy from me gold refined in the fire, so that you can become rich; and white clothes to wear, so that you can cover your shameful nakedness; and salve to put on your eyes, so that you can see.

The city of Laodicea was completely *destroyed by an earthquake in 60M AD.* When the *emperor* offered Roman financial assistance to rebuild, the citizens of Laodicea were so *pridefully self-sufficient.* They refused his offer. *They rebuilt the city by themselves.*

- They were known as producers of the famous Laodicean *black wool* for clothing.
- They were the banking and financial center of the area.
- And they had medical facilities. They had access to Phrygia eye ointments called the Phrygian powder.

So what did they need? *Nothing! Absolutely nothing!*

Like the city citizens, the church had become *overconfident* in regard to their *spiritual wealth.* So much that they had failed to see their own spiritual bankruptcy.

They were so prideful of their *self-sufficiency...*

- that they could not see their need *to be continually washed in the blood of the Lamb...*
- they had become unaware of their dependency on *the power of Jesus working in their lives...daily!*

It was John who said, "If we claim to be without sin, we deceive ourselves and the truth is not in us...but if we confess our sins, He is faithful and just and will forgive us our sins and purify us from all unrighteousness... If we walk in the light, as he is in the light, we have fellowship with one another. the blood of Jesus, his Son, purifies us from all sin."

Is it possible for an individual or church to become caught up in its own *self-righteousness* that they forget the need for the cleansing power of *Jesus's blood? Evidently so... It was the problem in Laodicea!*

People, we must never think that we are saved by our own righteousness!

An Old Testament prophet tells us our *righteous acts of goodness* is nothing but *filthy rags* in the sight of God.

We need *white garments, garments made pure, cleansed* by the *forgiving, justifying, and saving* blood of Jesus. Otherwise, we are in spiritual nakedness...spiritual shame and worthlessness. If we don't *internalize* and *act* upon these facts, Jesus tells us we become *spiritually blind,* living in *spiritual darkness.*

For us to grow, we must *never, never* get to the point that...

- *we depend upon our own moral goodness* for righteousness
- we must never become *addicted to our own salvation by works*
- like the praying Pharisee, we must never *see ourselves better than others*
- we must never lose sight of *our total dependency upon Jesus*

You see, we begin our Christian life *spiritually bankrupt*. As we grow, we understand even more *the depth of our sin* and our great need to be *clothed in the righteousness of our Savior*.

Church growth must begin with the understanding that...

- we can't do it by ourselves. *We need Jesus.* We're saved by his righteousness, not our own
- we need God's *presence and power* working within us

Based upon these thoughts, allow me to make some *practical suggestions* for our continued growth as God's family.

We must continue to be *faithful to God's Word*.

Evidently, the church in Laodicea made some changes. There was a *council of churches* held in Laodicea around 361 to 364 AD. The primary objective of which was to determine what was *cannon*... What books were to be considered as Scripture for the family of God? In this council, *they authorized as scripture* all but one New Testament book we hold in our hands today.

We must create interest in Jesus by *living out His principles daily*.

In John chapter 1, when Jesus was asked by John's disciples, "Where are You staying?" He replied, "Come see... Come see."

People, our future growth is going to be directly proportional to our allowing others...our children, extended family, friends, neighbors, working companions, and others we meet...*to see Jesus in us... Do they? Really?*

Seeing Christ lived out in us daily creates interest!

We must be focused upon Jesus...*focused on salvation issues*

- Faith
- Repentance...a changed life
- Confession of both His Deity and humanity
- And on the new birth...baptism for remission of sins and the gift of God's presence

You see, church growth occurs when we are *focused on Jesus*. Remember, it is God who adds to the church, not mankind!

Controversial issues cause division! Faith in Jesus causes growth! It was the Hebrews writer who admonished to *keep your eyes upon Jesus.*

We must meet and greet every new face in our gatherings.

First impressions are important. When a visitor enters our building for a worship service or fellowship event, we must let them know they're welcome. Greet them with a smile and warm conversation.

We must be willing to *serve and save* the community.

God works through His people. It was Christ who said, "As often as you do it *to the least...to the least...*of these...you do it unto Me."

We must be *enthusiastic* about our faith.

This letter from Jesus tells us that *lukewarmness* breeds more apathy...and *apathy* brings certain death to churches. We must never allow this to overtake us individually or as a body of believers.

We must let others know there's a *ministry for them* in our church family.

Jesus describes the kingdom of God in terms of *work.* He uses parables that speak of *the church* as a *field, a vineyard, and a business of building, buying, and selling.*

We must *find our own place in ministry.*

- Being faithful is *more* than coming to services.
- Christianity is *more* than Sunday worship.
- Christianity is *not* a spectator sport.
- It's *not* even an avocation but a *way to live* in service...in ministry to Him.

Here is a sobering question: Are we working in His kingdom... or just attending services?

Well, note if you will read verse 20, hear Jesus say, "Here I am! I stand at the door and knock. If anyone hears my voice and opens the door...I will come in and eat with him, and he with me."

We as individuals must all work together to start a program at our church to win souls and get the people that have left the church to come back and make our churches count again.

New Testament Evangelism

Acts 2:41–47, 8:4–8

The book of Acts is a thrilling story about the birth of Christianity and its explosive expansion from Jerusalem to Judea to Samaria into Asia Africa to Europe and the uttermost parts of the earth.

Paul tells us in Colossians 1:23 that the Early Church took the Gospel to their world in a single generation. *Can you believe that!* What a feat for the primitive church… What a goal for us in our generation, *right?*

What was the secret of this excitement, this enthusiasm, and this extraordinary growth? How do we explain their success? How did they accomplish it?

I believe the book of Acts contains our answer! Acts is our manual on church growth. Growth made possible through genuine New Testament evangelism. Although the word *evangelism* does not occur in our English translations, the spirit of *evangelism* flows from every page.

I believe we can replicate their same results today if we will have their *mentality*. If we will preach their *message* and adhere to their *model*.

First, like them, we must be sure of our purpose.

These first Christians knew that their mission was to *go make disciples!* Evangelism was their business! Their reason for existence!

I believe it significant that the first symbol of Christianity was not the cross...but the tongue! It was the symbol chosen by God on Pentecost. Every baptized believer should be ready to *talk* about the Savior! "But, Brother, I don't know how to talk to my neighbor!" Invite him to church where they can *hear* the Gospel taught and preached. According to a survey of ten thousand people by the Institute for Church Growth, 79 percent said they were led to Christ *because a friend invited them to church!*

Church, are we as serious about our purpose as we should be?

Secondly, we must have an evangelistic consciousness.

The early Christians were *opportunist*. They were constantly looking for openings to communicate the good news about Jesus to others.

Of the sixty evangelistic encounters in Acts, at least a third developed spontaneously without deliberate arranging from a human standpoint.

- In Acts 3, Peter and John healed a beggar at the temple. When a curious crowd of spectators assembled to see the man who had been healed, Peter seized the opportunity to preach to them with great success.
- When persecution scattered first Christians over the Mediterranean world, they turned their exile into an evangelistic opportunity.
- In Philippi, Paul and Silas took advantage of an earthquake to evangelize a Roman jailer and his family.

We too must learn to allow evangelism to color the casual contacts of daily life.

Folks, is it possible that God providentially brings people into our lives for the specific purpose of our communicating Jesus to them verbally or by example?

- People like the girl at the grocery store
- The teller at the bank
- Our golfing companions, etc.

Today, we think that evangelism is a matter of aptitude, the right training, or expertise; when in reality, what matters most is *attitude!*

God helps us exploit each and every opportunity He brings our way, *right?*

A few years ago, a Gallup Poll revealed that 50 percent of the unchurched in our nation see themselves as becoming active church members. That same poll indicated that 80 percent of these people wanted their children to have religious training.

Friends, the world is filled with people to save. We must believe that the power to save them is in the Gospel message.

We must have a biblical concept of success.

Many of us feel that we have failed when we confront others with the truth about Jesus without converting them to Christ, *so we've stopped trying.* But the book of Acts measures success by faithfulness in sowing, not by the size of the harvest.

Repeatedly we are told in Acts of efforts which produced *no* harvest of souls.

- Some reacted to the good news with angry hostility.
- Some even killed the messenger.
- Others wanted to know more.

But early Christians knew their role and our task was to sow the seed…to plant and water…while leaving the result, the harvest, to God.

We must have an urgency for souls.

Soon after his conversion, we find Saul of Tarsus already at work preaching the Gospel. This spirit of urgency can also be seen in the account of Peter and John's response to the Sanhedrin not to teach or preach at all in the name of Jesus. They said, "We cannot stop speaking what we have seen and heard."

Remember Saul's response to the Macedonian call? *And when he had seen the vision, immediately we sought to go into Macedonia.*

We will never duplicate their achievements as long as we are convinced that there is plenty of time and that there is no hurry.

Then, we must have a spirit of submission.

Jesus commanded them and us. *Go into the world. Preach the Gospel to every creature. Go make disciples of every tuition. And I will be with you always.*

They were determined to obey God completely. Recently, I read a survey of those who attended services three times a week.

- Only 59 percent felt that they had any responsibility to tell others about Jesus.
- Twenty-seven percent actually disagreed with the whole concept of evangelism.

We're better Bible students than to think like this. We *know* that we ought to be sharing the good news of Jesus with others.

The direct command from Jesus is *into all the world...to every creature...and I will be with you always...the command and the promise:*

- The command is to go tell others.
- The promise is I will be with you always.

Ironic, isn't it? We want the promise, but we reject the command.

Not only must we have an apostolic mentality, *we must preach their message.*

Apostolic preaching must be *centered on the cross.*

An analysis of early Christian preaching shows repeated references to the reality of Calvary. Paul seems to speak for all when he said, "I was determined to know nothing except Jesus Christ and Him crucified... We preach Christ crucified... The power and the wisdom of God."

You see, God's whole scheme of grace and redemption hangs upon the cross. No doctrine is sound, which does not have its roots in the *cross.* Modem preaching may promote many true things, even some helpful things, but it is *powerless* to save if it' s not centered upon the cross.

Like theirs, our message must be one of conviction.

The apostles preached with *authority and conviction.* So must we! *So must we!* They never compromised their message.

They preached

- the sinfulness of mankind
- the lost condition of the unsaved
- the fearful reality of God's promised judgment

They did not shrink from declaring the *whole* counsel of God, even the face of persecution.

They preached a message of hope and resurrection.

I believe *hope* and the *resurrection* go inseparably together. There is no hope *without* the resurrection. Have you ever counted the sermons that mention the resurrection?

- The first sermon of Pentecost: "Let all Israel be assured of this… God has made this Jesus, whom you crucified, both Lord and Christ."

Peter's sermon at the beautiful gate: "You killed the author of life… But God raised him from the dead."

- Paul preached resurrection: "For God has set a day when he will judge the world with justice by the man he has appointed. He has given proof of this to all men by raising him from the dead."

Apart from the resurrection, there is good news to proclaim.

Our message must demand a response.

Apostolic preaching had an explosive result on audiences.

- Some rejoiced.
- Some resisted.

But none simply ignored.

Of the more than sixty evangelistic encounters in Acts, at least two-thirds of them produced a favorable response.

- In Iconium, the city was divided by the preaching of Paul and Barnabas.
- In Thessalonica, a great multitude of Greeks and leading men were converted. But the Jews rioted.
- In Berea, many Jews believed… But others stirred a mob into a frenzy against the apostles.
- In Athens, some sneered… But others believed.
- At Corinth, many believed… But others brought Paul before the judgment seat.

Sometimes, in our desire to *not* be *offensive*, we can cease to be *effective*. A craving for respectability and popularity can make our preaching less than it ought to be. You see, if we are to achieve apostolic results we must go to the world with an *apostolic message*. We must confront people with the truth about Jesus.

The third concept we want to address is, we must adhere to the apostolic model found in Acts chapter 1.

We must know the scriptures.

The book of Acts starts with a Bible study. *After His suffering, He showed Himself to these men and gave many convincing proofs that he was alive. He appeared to them over a period of forty days and spoke about the kingdom of God.* Genuine New Testament evangelism demands we be a people of the book.

We must anticipate his coming.

After he said this, he was taken before their very eyes, and a cloud hid him from their sight. They were looking intently up into the sky as he was going when suddenly two men dressed in white stood beside them. "Men of Galilee," they said, "why do you stand here looking into the sky? This same Jesus, who has been taken from you into heaven, will come back in the same way you have seen him go into heaven."

This angelic message rang in the ears of those who witnessed this event for the rest of their lives.

- These people wanted and waited for Him to return.
- They prayed for His return.
- They lived in anticipation of the second corning.

Do we really expect him to come? *Do we?* Do we expect His to return?

- Before we die?
- This year?
- How about tomorrow?
- Before this book is concluded?

Here it is. The early church was evangelistic because *they expected Jesus to return in their lifetime...maybe today...maybe today!*

And I am convinced we'll be more diligent in teaching our children, our neighbors, and friends when we come to accept the truth. *That Jesus is coming...maybe soon!*

Then finally, we must follow their model of qualified leadership.

I believe that one of the greatest deterrents to church growth today is a lack of leadership. In the closing verses of Acts chapter 1, Judas had only been dead forty days...and they were already selecting one to replace him.

I think this points out God's focus...God's desire for proper leadership in our churches.

The problem facing the church today is...

- Not a lack of power in the Gospel
- The blood of Christ has not been diluted
- Nor is the work of the Holy Spirit through the word any less effective.

The problem is us.

You see, church growth...genuine New Testament evangelism is an outgrowth of *genuine conversion.*

Have we been converted or are we just church members? Pew sitters? Spectators?

Sobering questions for any church that claims to be the church established at Pentecost.

Give us a watchword for the hour,
A thrilling word…a word of power,
A battle cry…a flaming breath,
A call to conquest or to death,
A word to wake the church from rest,
To heed the Master's high request.

The call is given, ye hosts arise,
The watchword is *evangelize*,
To fallen man, a dying race,
Make known the gift of Gospel grace.
The world now in darkness lies.
O dear church, "Evangelize!"

Perhaps as a child of God, we have stumbled in our walk…and instead of contributing to the growth of the Lord's church, we have held it back. Come making this right with God and right with your brothers and sister in Christ.

Expanding Growth Principles

Acts 3:1–13, 16; 4:4, 13

Change.

- It's easier to stay in our comfort zone...doing what we've always done...rather than consider that we live in a *changing world*.
- And admitting that *past accomplishments* are no guarantee of *future growth*.

Now you're *not* hearing me say we must change.

- Gospel message
- The New Testament pattern of worship
- Church organization and government
- Or our focus on biblical authority

But I am saying that there are some paradigm shifts that we *can and should embrace* in order to expand the kingdom.

We noted how the Jerusalem church started with three thousand souls on Pentecost. Later we note the adding of five thousand *new souls* from an incident in Acts chapter 3.

Peter and John are on their way to the temple for the three o'clock prayer service when they encounter a man whom everybody knew had been crippled from birth. He was brought to the Temple gate to beg from those attending the daily prayer services. Peter says, "Silver and gold I don't have, but what I do have I give you... In the Name of Jesus...*walk!* Instantly His feet and ankles became strong and he began to walk, entering the temple courts praising God, and the people were filled with wonder and amazement.

The people assumed that Peter and John had healed this cripple by their own power. But Peter says, "Don't you suppose for a moment that this was accomplished by our own power or godliness? The God of Abraham... Isaac and Jacob has made him whole."

Then he calls on them to do the same as those on Pentecost... *Repent and turn to God so that your sins may be wiped out and that times of refreshing may come from the Lord.*

When they saw the courage of Peter and John and realized that they were unschooled, ordinary men, they were astounded and took note that these men had been with Jesus.

Come, let's see what we can learn about *church growth* in today's world.

What *paradigm shifts* must we be willing to make?

First, church growth is a result of our being a people and person of right motive.

Motive is doing the right thing for the right reason. When I say *pure motive*, I want us to contrast Peter and John here...with Ananias and Sapphira... Just two more chapters over in Acts 5. In the Sermon on the Mount, Jesus repeatedly warns against doing our acts of righteousness...*giving alms, praying, and fasting* for the wrong reason and out of an improper motive.

Today, the people of the whole world are watching *us* for *motive!*

Motive! Motive! People can see quickly if we are doing our religion for the wrong reason or not.

For instance, they are turned off...

- when we start talking about what great things *we've* done *in or for* the church...

- when we use the big I as we brag about good deeds done, good works preformed, sermons preached, classes taught, church growth, and missions.

Question, can our children, friends, neighbors, and working companions *see Jesus in us...or are they seeing us in us?* Church growth is *not* about us and our inventive schemes but about God working in us through faith.

In verse 11, when Peter and John sensed that the people of Jerusalem thought they were responsible for this man's healing, Peter asked, "Why do you *stare at us* as if by our power or godliness we made this man to walk?"

Verse 16 gives us the proper motive: "A faith in Jesus has healed this man."

You see, church growth occurs in two ways, spiritually and numerically...*and it's God's decision* which and to what extent this growth will occur.

- It was Paul who made the point in the Corinthian Church... I planted, Apollos watered, but God gave increase. He who plants, waters, and cultivates are nothing... But God who gives the increase.
- In Colossians, he points out that Jesus is head of the church. And He is the one who *makes it grow.*
- Jesus said in John chapter 15, "I am the Vine... You are the branches... My Father God is the Gardener. He is responsible for growth... Apart from Me...you can do nothing."
- David gave us this principle three thousand years ago... Unless the Lord builds the house, its builders labor in vain.

You see, it's possible for us to be the church of God anywhere... and *not* grow numerically. However, we must be willing to allow *God to work His will in our lives*...corporately as a church and individually. Ours is to focus on becoming God's people and person by living out our religion daily as did the early church... By living for Jesus with right motive and leave the growth to God.

Today, people are interested in churches that see themselves as *God's family*...governed by biblical principles... Not a business to be run on modern-day business principles.

Secondly, church growth occurs when we understand that our religion is more than a Sunday morning ritual.

We can't help noticing two things in this narrative:

- Christianity is more than a Sunday affair.

Peter and John were involved with worshipping God on a daily basis.

- Plus, we note that there seems to be a *relationship between the churches, the Christian, children of God, and helping others.*
- *More than a Sunday morning habit*
- *More than coming to church.*

It was James who wrote, "Pure religion...religion that God accepts...is this...to look after orphans and widows in their distress and to keep oneself from being polluted by the world."

In Ephesians 2, we find that God created us and saved us by grace and faith *to do good works.*

We noted that the first thought from Zacchaeus following his conversion in Luke chapter 19 was his responsibility to others, especially those he had wronged.

In Matthew 25, Jesus said that those on the right and left in Judgment will be separated according to their involving themselves in the lives of those in need.

Ask around. Check it out. Today, the religious organizations that are growing numerically or spiritually *are those involved in serving the Jesus in others.*

The third paradigm shift is that *we be willing to be interrupted.*

Our world is so caught up in scheduling that we seldom respond well to *interruptions.* But some of our most *useful moments* in God's kingdom are *those that are impromptu and unplanned.*

Did you know this? Of the sixty evangelistic encounters recorded in the book of Acts, one-third of them were *unplanned, impromptu* moments? Moments where God brings His people, *us*, into contact with others who are in need... And we *interrupt and serve*. Be it with the Gospel message or some other seen need.

In Jesus's narrative of the Good Samaritan, the priest and the Levi were doing good. They, like Peter and John, were on their way *to or from* temple worship. But they were *unwilling to be interrupted...* and Jesus condemned them.

Jesus is our example. *He went about doing good.*

- At Jacob's well, Jesus takes time to have the longest discussion He has with any one individual recorded in the Scripture... And that conversation resulted in a whole community being converted.
- After a busy day, He took time for Nicodemus.
- Jesus was willing to be interrupted by children.
- He interrupted His preaching ministry to attend the funeral of a friend at Bethany.
- He took time to visit with Mary in the garden.

Indeed!

Our most useful kingdom moments...our most successful evangelistic moments are the impromptu ones... Those providentially provided by God when we are willing to be interrupted for the sake of the kingdom.

Seriously, we must ask ourselves, are we *too busy* to become God's instrument of righteousness? Too busy for God to use us in the life of this person and his or her need?

Today's church must be willing to see *what other's choose to ignore.*

Remember the incident where Jesus was leaving the temple in John chapter 9?

Like Peter and John, he was confronted by someone in need... *by a blind man.*

- Now, the people saw this man every day. To them, he had just become another *fixture* at the temple gate. They failed to see his hurt.
- The Pharisees saw a problem with healing on the Sabbath.
- The apostles saw a theological question about who sinned... this man or his parents?
- *Jesus saw a person in need...and a chance to let God's glory be seen in him...through him!!*

What would we have seen had we been there with Jesus that day? More importantly, *what do we see in our world today?*

The Hebrews writer sobers our thinking with this statement: *Do not forget to entertain strangers, for by so doing some people have entertained angels without knowing it.*

Today, people are looking for those willing to inspire hope in others.

In verse 5, this lame beggar looked at Peter and John *expecting something.*

The world is looking at us in church...this church...*expecting...*

- great
- good
- tender
- loving
- merciful
- forgiving

Attitudes and behavior

They expect us to have the heart, the mind, the attitude, disposition, and behavior of Jesus.

- What will we show them?
- What will we give them?

Growing churches are those who keep their eyes and hearts focused upon Jesus and how we can serve him by serving others.

We must be willing to use what we have.

God has blessed us with many blessings…money, education, knowledge of the Word, our homes, cars, etc. I have people say to me, *Well, if…*

- If I had more money…
- If I had more time…
- If I had more energy…
- If I was better equipped…
- If I had better health…
- If I were younger…

If…If…

Before the burning bush, Moses said, "*I can't… I don't have the equipment.*" God said, "*What is that in your hand?*"

The apostles said, "We don't have enough to feed this crowd." Jesus said, "What *do* you have?"

Peter said, "*I don't have what you want… But I have what you need… In the name of Jesus, arise and walk.*"

We cannot wait. We have everything *just right. They need Jesus now!* And some are waiting on Him to invite them, welcome them, serve them, and teach them. *Amen?*

Another paradigm shift is our understanding that God will work through our faith in Him.

I think I can remember a time in the church where we thought God did not providentially supply us with what we need to do His work in the world… *But He does!*

- In Ephesians 321, Paul tells us *the power of God is at work in us.*
- The Hebrews writer ends his letter by saying, "*God will equip you with everything good for doing His will.*"
- Philippians has Paul saying, "*I can do all things through Jesus who strengthens me. Being confident of this, that he who began a good work in you will carry it to completion, until the end, of Jesus.*"

93

Think about this, see if it is not true, the *dominant characteristic* of those people God uses in the Bible, either individually or collectively, *are men and woman of faith?*

One of the most exciting stories ever to come out of my work with Gospel tracts is one about a lady who is a member of a local congregation. She sent a tract with a Bible lesson to a student in West Africa. *Seven years later,* a man found that tract blowing down the streets of Ghana. He picked it up, read it, and was into Christ.

Folk, we must do *what we can do* and trust God for the rest… Trust God for the growth.

One more idea that we must embrace: God uses ordinary men, women, and teens.

Look at the last verse of this text: When they saw the courage of Peter and John and realized that they were *unschooled, ordinary* men, they were astonished and they took note that these men had been with Jesus.

We don't have to be someone special for God to use us. All that's required is that *we be willing to spend time with Jesus.*

- Submit to His will… His commands.
- Have His heat, His altitude, disposition, act react to life as did Jesus.
- Conform to His image…follow His example.

Are we willing? I pray that we are.

Notice the *results* when ordinary people.
People of the pew are willing to be used of God.
Verse 4 of chapter 4: "Many who heard the message believed… And the number of men grew to about five thousand."
Let me close by sharing some sobering statements with you that I discovered this week.
Just listen and allow them to soak in.

- Growing churches are always spending more than their income… Dead churches have no need for more money.

94

- Growing churches have parking problems... Dead churches have empty spaces.
- Growing churches have noisy children... Dead churches are as quiet as a cemetery.
- Growing churches keep changing what needs to be changed to reach the lost... Dead churches have no need to change.
- Growing congregations have trouble keeping up with people's names... Dead churches know everybody's name... and all their sins.
- Growing churches have an active mission and evangelistic outreach... Dead churches have a healthy bank account.
- Growing churches move ahead on prayer and faith... Dead churches have no need for either... They walk and work by sight.
- Active churches outgrow their Bible school facilities... Dead churches have room to spare.
- Growing churches welcome all classes of people. Dead churches stick to their own kind.
- Growing church members look for someone they can help... Dead church members look for something to complain about.
- Alive church members share their faith... Dead members don't have enough to share.
- Growing churches enthusiastically support their ministries... Dead churches have no ministries...only functions.

If you read this and want to become a part of a church committed to *spiritual and numerical* growth, the invitation is yours by...

- a faith in Jesus
- a commitment to a changed, like Jesus, lifestyle
- and by New Testament baptism

Growth Encouragement Factor

First Thessalonians 5.11, 14; 2 Thessalonians 2:17
Second Timothy 4:2; Titus 1:9; Hebrews 3:13, 10:25

Let me give you the lesson in a sentence. Church growth flourishes in an atmosphere of encouragement... *Church growth flourishes in an atmosphere of encouragement.*

You'll need a Bible. Open it to Acts chapter 4.

It is interesting to note that there are *over one hundred one another passages* in the New Testament.

- We are to care for one another.
- Teach and admonish one mother.
- Bear one another's burdens.
- Serve one another.
- Be kind one to another.
- Prefer one another.
- Be hospitable to one another.
- Forgive one another.
- Live at peace with one another.
- Pray for one another.
- And encourage one another.

Encouragement... We all need it!

- Families need encouragement.
- Our children need encouragement.
- The sick and suffering need encouragement.
- Senior citizen need encouragement.
- Lost souls need encouragement.
- Individual Christians need encouragement.
- Churches committed to growth need encouragement.
- You and I need it!

Actually, the word *encourage* or *encouragement* does not appear in our King James Bibles, but when we consult the New International Version, we find the following *challenges* from Scripture.

First Thessalonians 5:11, 14 states, "Therefore encourage one another and build each other up, just as in fact you are doing. Encourage the timid. Help the weak. Be patient with everyone."

Second Thessalonians 2:17 states, "Be encouraged in your hearts and strengthened in every good deed and word."

Second Timothy 4:2 states, "Preach the Word; be prepared in season and out of season; correct, rebuke and encourage, with great patience and careful instruction."

Titus 1:9 states, "Hold firmly to the trustworthy message as it has been taught, so that we can encourage others by sound doctrine and refute those who oppose it."

Hebrews 3:13 states, "Encourage one another daily, as long as it is called today, so that none of you may be hardened by sin's deceitfulness."

Hebrews 10:25 states, "Forsake not the assembling of yourselves together, as the habit of some has become. but let us encourage one another—and all the more as see the day approaching."

With these Scriptures in mind, let's see what we can learn about becoming *encouragers* as we strive to *grow God's church.*

I believe God has placed in scripture a definition... *No! More than a definition...a model* for us to follow. We find our *definition* and *model* in the book of Acts.

Our model has three names...

- *Joseph*
- Called *Barnabas*
- And his nickname is *son of encouragement.*
- Our King James says *son of consolation.*

What I want to do with the lesson is simply *scan the book of Acts* and see what we can learn from this *one* known as the *son of encouragement.*

Turn to Acts chapter 4. Beginning with the verse numbered 32 (emphasis added) where we meet Barnabas for the first time.

> All the believers were one in heart and mind. No-one claimed that any of his possessions was his own, but they shared everything they had. With great power the apostles continued to testify to the resurrection of the Lord Jesus, and much grace was upon them all. There were no needy persons among them. For from time to time those who owned lands or houses sold them, brought the money from the sales and put it at the apostles' feet, and it was distributed to anyone as he had need. Joseph, a Levite from Cyprus, whom the apostles called Barnabas... *which means son of encouragement...* Sold afield he owned and brought the money and put it at the apostles' feet.

So what are the characteristics of an encourager?
First, an encourager gives freely of their resources.

Barnabas sells a piece of land and gives the money to the church, and they distribute it to those who are in need. The New Testament church of the first century had *a family mind-set.* They believed in and practiced the idea of *what is mine is mine but it is yours if you need it.*

This idea came from John the Baptist. It was a part of his message of *repentance*. He said, "The kingdom of God is coming... Prepare for it by repentance." Then he told what repentance was. I think we need to read *Luke 3:11* again. Perhaps we have forgotten the message.

When asked what repentance was, John answered, "The man with two coats should share with him who has none, and the one who has food should do the same."

John is saying that New Testament *churches, Christians, and kingdom seekers* will be known as *people of encouragement*...those willing to share...those willing to *give to others in need.*

And they were. The book of Acts bears this out repeatedly, *right?*

Encouragement sometimes means (1) giving to others and (2) fulfilling the needs of others *out of our own God-given resources.*

You see, encouragers recognize that what we have really doesn't belong to us at all but to God. *We are only stewards of God's blessings.*

All too frequently, we live as if we will take our possessions with us... *We won't!*

- There are no pockets in funeral shrouds.
- Hearses don't pull U-Hauls.

Barnabas understood this. Evidently he didn't need this field... *this second coat.* But some of his brethren did... So he freely gives to others.

Sometimes words are not enough?

James says it's not enough when a brother comes needing help for us to say "I wish you well" or "Go your way" or "Be you warmed and filled."

We must back up our words with tangible encouragement...support.

Church growth begins...

- when we are willing to *freely give of our tangible resources* God has given us
- when we are willing to share our blessings

Another point here, encouragers give with an open-hand philosophy. When they give, it's over. It is a done deal.

- *They're not looking for anything in return.*
- *They could care less who gets the credit.*

Their main goal is simply *to meet the need.*

Barnabas sells the property and simply gives the proceeds to the apostles *for them to distribute...no strings attached.* Barnabas was *not,* is not found saying. *I'll give this...if you'll spend it as I want...as I direct.*

Corrie Ten Boom put it so well when she said, "I've learned not to hold on to anything too tightly, because it hurts too much when God has to pry back my fingers to get to it. So I've learned to live life with an open hand so that God can give and take as he wishes."

That was Job's philosophy, wasn't it? *The Lord gives...the Lord takes.* May God help us to be like Barnabas, *an encourager* with an open heart and hand.

I want you to notice what happens *when we share our God-given resources with others,* including sharing the truth about Jesus and His resurrection. What does Luke say happened? *And much grace was upon them all.*

How many of us want and need more of God's grace in our life? Then Scripture says *become an encourager!*

Become an Encourager

Thirdly, an encourager accepts us where we are.

Turn to Acts chapter 9. The Jews were in a conspiracy to kill Paul. But fellow church members slipped him out of town by night in a basket over the wall. He then goes to Jerusalem to join with the church there, *but they were afraid of him.* They couldn't believe he had been converted to Jesus.

After all, they had seen him there holding the coats who stoned Stephen. Perhaps they had witnessed others being *jailed, beaten, or killed* because of Paul's efforts in ravaging the church of Christ.

Acts 9:21 says, "Isn't this the man who caused havoc in Jerusalem among those who call on this name? And hasn't he come here to take them as prisoners to the chief priests?"

These Christians in Jerusalem had reason for concern, *didn't they?*

But notice who comes to the rescue.

Let your eyes fall to 9:27: "But Barnabas took him and brought him to the Apostles and told them about his Damascus road experience. So Paul stayed in Jerusalem, moving about freely, Speaking boldly in the name of Jesus."

Do you see our next characteristic of an encourager?

Encouragers *accept us where we are, helping us to be what we can be.*

Encouragers don't look at our *past but at the present and future possibilities.*

Encouragers don't spend their time examining our *faults and mistakes, our sins, but noting our potential...what we could be.*

You see, as His children, as baptized believers, if *God doesn't hold our past against us,* who are we to hold one another's past against each other? *In Christ* we are *new creatures...a new creation...* Old things have passed away. Behold all things have been made new.

Jesus is the example here.

Let me show you. *The heart, the attitude, disposition, and behavior* of an encourager from the life of Jesus.

First there's Simon Peter.

Why would Jesus call Peter to be apostle? Why would Jesus select such an individual into His inner circle of intimacy...made up of Peter, James, and John?

- Didn't Jesus foresee that Peter would take his eyes off Him and sink into the Sea of Galilee?
- Didn't Jesus know that Peter would ultimately deny Him and forsake Him in his hour of need?

There's Matthew.

Matthew was a tax Collector, one who was focused on materialism...one who gained his material abundance on the backs of his fellow countryman, *Jews.* A most unlikely disciple of Jesus. But Matthew emerges as one of Jesus's most promising followers. He would go on to write the First Gospel... Written to the very Jews he once cheated.

Then we note the *woman at the well.*

Jesus sees the potential in a woman who has ruined her life with five husbands and a live-in. But with encouragement, because Jesus accepted her where she was, she becomes an evangelist responsible for converting the entire city of Sychar.

There's the adulterous woman in John chapter 8.

Here Jesus tells a sinner, "Go your way and sin no more."

- Was Jesus saying "It's not your fault... You're not guilty"? *No.* By His very words, He authenticates her guilt.
- Was he saying "Adultery is not a bad sin"? *No!*

Jesus is saying "I came to call sinners to repentance. *I see your sin. I forgive you.* Now go start building a better life. Just do it. *I believe in you.*"

What a difference do you suppose we can we make in the lives of

- our children
- our neighbors
- those in the church of God
- the lost
- and those we differ with religiously

If we will just *accept them where they are* while *helping them* get where they should be rather *judging them on their past or their present?* Encouragers don't see what we *are...but what we could be.* *Encouragers get excited about the progress and potential of others.* Turn to Acts 11 and read beginning with verse numbered 19.

> Now those had been scattered by the persecution in connection with Stephen who traveled as far as Phoenicia, Cyprus and Antioch, telling the message only to Jews. Some of them, however, men from Cyprus and Cyrene, went to Antioch and began to speak to Greeks also, telling them the good news about the Lord Jesus. The Lord's hand was with them, and a great number of people believed and turned to the Lord. News of this reached the ears of the church at Jerusalem, and they sent Barnabas to Antioch. When he arrived and saw the evidence of the grace of God, he was glad and encouraged them all to remain true to the Lord with all their hearts. He was a good man, full of the Holy Spirit and faith, and a great number of people were brought to the Lord. Then Barnabas went to Tarsus to look for Saul, and when he found him, he brought him to Antioch. So for a whole year Barnabas and Saul

met with the church and taught great numbers of people. The disciples were called Christians first at Antioch.

Did you notice what Barnabas did in *verse 23?* He was glad at their *conversion and encouraged* them to remain true to the Lord He got excited about their *progress.*

Encouragers get excited about the *progress of others.* For instance,

- When they see a Christian overcome temptation and some ugly sin in their life. *They encourage them and rejoice with them.*
- When they see parents raising their children in the nurture and admonition of the Lord, *they encourage them.*
- When they see church members involved in genuine New Testament evangelism, *they support them…encourage them.*
- When they see new converts growing and exercising their convictions from Scripture, *they praise and encourage them.*
- When they witness elders and pastor lovingly, tenderly shepherding the flock, *they support and encourage them.*

Personally, I believe we have too many in the church today.

- Looking for and pointing out problems.
- Checking for faults.
- Questioning our faith and practice.
- Criticizing elders
- Going about just generally being *mean spirited and ugly minded!*

What we need is more *encouragement* for everyone to be *true to the Lord.*

That's exactly what Barnabas did.

I want you to note what happens when believers are *encouraged to be true to the Lord.* Look at verses 24 through 26.

- Great numbers of people were taught.
- Great numbers of people were brought to the Lord.
- And they were called Christians first at Antioch.

Church growth is a of *what? Encouragement! Encouragement. Number five, encouragers are unselfish.*

Things were going well in the church at Antioch. But, here in Acts 11, Barnabas goes to Tarsus for Paul.

That's strange thinking for us today… When things are going well, *we want to…*

- *take all the credit*
- *ride the success train as far as we can…not Barnabas!*

He knew that Paul could do a much better job in *growing* the church at Antioch. Barnabas knew that he had brought this church as far as he could without help.

So he strikes out for assistance.

You see…

- Encouragers are not out to make a name for themselves but are interested in church growth.
- Encouragers are willing to take a back seat when another person can do a better job.
- Encouragers are willing to preach in small churches.
- Encouragers teachers are willing to teach even if there is only one student in the class.
- Encouragers have a servant mentality.
- Encouragers are willing to wash feet.
- Encouragers are willing to place the good of others before their preferences.
- Encouragers are those who are willing to hold up the hands of others.

- Encouragers are those willing to send others on foreign missions when they can't go.

Church growth is not about us... But about us seeing the potential in others and being humble enough, unselfish enough to allow others to use their abilities.

Then finally, encouragers give others a second chance.

In Acts 15:36–41, Paul and Barnabas decide to go back and visit the churches they planted on the first missionary journey...*but there is a problem.*

What's the problem? More correctly, *who* is the problem? *It was John Mark.* Barnabas wants to give John Mark *a second chance.*

You remember that he deserted them on the first mission trip and returned home from Cyprus...about one-third of the way through the evangelist effort.

Paul says, "No! He isn't a going!" Barnabas says, "Paul, he deserves another chance." Scripture tells us the disagreement was so sharp that Paul and Barnabas *split company.*

- Paul chose *Silas.*
- Barnabas takes *John Mark.*

And they each set out on separate journeys.

There is an interesting reason as to *why Barnabas stood up for John Mark*, giving him a *second chance.* I don't know if it is true or not...but it could be.

You remember in Acts chapter 1? Judas has hanged himself and the apostles are selecting another to take his place. Two men were selected... *Matthias* and *Joseph Barsabbas.* They cast lots and *Matthias* was selected.

Is it possible that *Joseph Barsabbas* was really *Joseph Barnabas?* Had the apostles, the disciples, or the early church changed his name to *Barnabas* because of his *encouragement of others?* If so, perhaps we can understand why Barnabas was so sensitive to John Mark's *rejection.* He knew the pain of *failure and rejection* firsthand.

Encouragers are willing to *give others a second chance.*

In this church family, we have preachers, leaders, deacons, ministry leaders, and people in the pew *who have failed?*

However... However... If we're going to grow...

- we must forgive them,
- give then another chance, and
- encourage them.

You see, the western world business model is *fire them.* Get somebody who can do the job. God's model is *give them another chance.*

Aren't you glad that *God is an encourager?*

Aren't we glad that he didn't give up on us at our first...second... third...hundredth...thousandth *failure...but keeps giving us another chance...another chance...and another chance?*

Peter says that He is not willing that any should perish but that all should come to repentance. *Indeed! God is an encourager.*

Well, the challenge is for us to be...

- more like Barnabas
- more like Jesus

Become encouragers...*because church growth flourishes in an atmosphere of encouragement.*

It's not hard and will not cost you anything except a little time, and you will have the time of your life. You just have to remember the golden rule and the rewards will last a lifetime. Be considerate and think of others. You will lay up stores in heaven and add stars to your crown. Win those souls! Bring 'em back and into the church, bring 'em back alive!

About the Author

Gary Vickery has been a Christian since September 21, 1964, so this should tell you that he is not a young man. He has tried to be the best Christian that he could be; however, just like Paul, he also has not been the Christian that he wanted to be each and every day of his life. He has always asked for forgiveness and repented; that is all any person can do, and with the grace of God, he is going to heaven.

Gary is a country boy, growing up in a small town in Alabama. He grew up in abject poverty with his mother and father and a total of ten children, two girls and eight boys. He was the seventh son in this family, so he was next to the last one, with his younger brother being the last child.

His father was the seventh son in his family, and he was the seventh son in his family and the only one of ten children to graduate high school. He also has a business degree from a four-year college.

He is retired from a life of working in a lumber business and now lives alone in Haleyville, Alabama. If for any reason you wish to talk to him, his email is garvic59@yahoo.com. Send him a message with your phone number, and he will call you back.

CPSIA information can be obtained
at www.ICGtesting.com
Printed in the USA
BVHW081322220421
605632BV00005B/551